JavaScript: Powering the Web. A Visual Guide to Interactive Web Pages

KRISTIAN B. SCHUSTER

Contents

Introduction: Welcome to the World of JavaScript – The Soul of the Web! 9

    What is JavaScript and Why is it Essential? – Beyond Static Pages 9

    JavaScript's Role in Web Development: The Dynamic Layer 9

    How This Book Will Help You: Visuals, Clear Code, and Practical Projects.............................. 10

    Setting Up Your Development Environment: Your Coding Workshop 10

Chapter 1: JavaScript Fundamentals: Your First Steps – Laying the Groundwork 11

    1.1 Writing Your First JavaScript Code: "Hello, World!" – Teaching the Web to Talk 11

        Why Is This Important? 13

    1.2 Understanding the <script> Tag: Inline vs. External Scripts – Connecting JavaScript to HTML 13

    1.3 Working with the Console: Debugging and Output – Your Secret Weapon for Web Development 14

        Accessing the Javascript Console 15

        Using the Console - The Key Functions 15

        Why Is This Important? 16

    1.4 Variables: Storing Data with Names – Giving Your Code a Memory 17

        Declaring Variables: let, const, and the Historical var 17

        Variable Naming Conventions: Readability Matters 18

        Assigning Values: Putting Data into Your Containers 19

    1.5 Data Types: Numbers, Strings, Booleans – Classifying the Information Your Code Handles 19

    Numbers: Representing the Quantitative World.. 20

    Strings: Representing Textual Data... 21

    Booleans: Representing Truth and Falsehood 22

    Conclusion: Data, Organized.. 23

Chapter 2: Making Your Pages Dynamic: Interacting with the DOM – Controlling the Webpage 24

    2.1 What is the DOM? The Document Object Model Explained – Your Code's Eye on the Webpage ... 24

        The DOM Tree: A Hierarchical View of Your Webpage 24

        Key Concepts of the DOM:... 25

        Accessing the DOM: JavaScript's Gateway 25

    Why the DOM Matters: Powering Dynamic Webpages 26

    2.2 Selecting Elements: getElementById, getElementsByClassName, querySelector – Finding the
    Pieces 26

    2.3 Modifying Element Content: innerHTML, textContent – Changing What the User Sees 28

        innerHTML: Powerful, but Potentially Perilous.. 28

textContent: Safe and Simple Text Replacement...29

A Final Thought 30

2.4 Changing Styles: style Property, Adding and Removing Classes – Altering the Appearance 30

2.5 Responding to Events: addEventListener – Listening and Reacting 31

Conclusion: Unlocking the Dynamic Web 32

Chapter 3: Controlling the Flow: Logic and Loops – Directing the Code's Path 33

3.1 Conditional Statements: if, else if, else – Making Decisions...................................33

3.2 Comparison Operators: ==, !=, >, <, >=, <= – Evaluating Conditions 34

3.3 Logical Operators: &&, ||, ! – Mastering the Art of Boolean Logic 35

Truthy and Falsy Values 37

3.4 Loops: for Loops – Automating Repetitive Tasks 38

The Anatomy of a for Loop: The Three Key Components 38

A Simple Example: Counting to Five 39

Example: Calculating with a Loop 40

Advanced: continue and break 40

Why Is This Important? 41

3.5 Loops: while Loops – Keep Going Until... 41

An Important First Principle! 41

Let's get more practical! 42

The importance of break and continue. 43

In Conclusion..44

Chapter 4: Working with Functions: Reusable Code Blocks – Your Key to Efficiency 44

4.1 Defining Functions: The function Keyword – Crafting Your Code's Workhorses...........................44

The Basic Structure of a Function 44

Where to put the functions?...46

4.2 Function Arguments: Passing Data to Functions – Giving Your Code a Voice 46

Parameters and Arguments: Defining the Terms 47

Functions with No Arguments 47

More Than One Argument 48

4.3 Returning Values: Getting Results from Functions – The Output of Your Code...........................49

Returning Multiple Values 50

Without the return Command!...50

In Conclusion 51

4.4 Scope: Local vs. Global Variables – Where Your Variables Can Be Seen 51

Local Scope: Inside the Function Walls 51

Global Scope: Visible Everywhere 52

Block Scope: 52

4.5 Anonymous Functions and Arrow Functions: Concise Syntax – Streamlining Your Code 53

Anonymous Functions: Quick and Ready 53

Arrow Functions: => 54

Chapter 5: Interacting with Users: Forms and Events – Listening to the World 56

5.1 Understanding HTML Forms: <form>, <input>, <button> – Gathering Information from Your Users
.... 56

The Foundation: The <form> Element 56

Gathering Information: The <input> Element 57

The Final Link: The <button> Element 58

5.2 Handling Form Submission: Preventing Default Behavior – Becoming the Gatekeeper 58

Understanding Default Form Submission 59

The Javascript Code 59

Here is a full function 60

5.3 Accessing Form Values: Getting User Input – Plucking Data From the Form 61

Setting Identifiers 61

Using getElementById to save data 61

Printing the Data Back 62

5.4 Validating Form Data: Ensuring Correct Input – Protecting the Data 63

Making a Good Look 64

5.5 Working with Events: click, submit, mouseover – Making Pages React! 64

Some Common Event Types 66

Conclusion: Your Bridge to the User 66

Chapter 6: Working with Arrays: Storing Collections of Data – Organizing Information 67

6.1 Creating Arrays: Different Methods – Assembling Your Collections 67

Method 1: Using Square Brackets – Easy and Efficient 67

Method 2: The new Array() Constructor (Less Common) 68

6.2 Accessing Array Elements: Indexing – Pointing to the Data You Need 68

Reading the Index 69

What to do with a longer list?..69

Summary of What to Do 70

6.3 Modifying Arrays: Adding, Removing, and Replacing Elements – Reshaping Your Data.................70

Addition of Elements...70

Removal of Elements 71

Replacing Elements 72

6.4 Array Methods: push, pop, shift, unshift, splice – Your Array Manipulation Arsenal....................73

1. Adding to the End: .push()..73

2. Removal from the End: .pop() 73

3. Adding to the Start: .unshift()..74

4. Removal from the Start: .shift()..74

5. The Swiss Army Knife: .splice() 74

6.5 Iterating Over Arrays: for Loops, forEach – Visiting Every Item in Your Collection 75

A simpler method: forEach loops. 76

Chapter 7: Working with Objects: Representing Real-World Entities – Modeling the World in Code.......78

7.1 Creating Objects: Object Literals – The Concise Way to Build Your Worlds.......................78

The Anatomy of an Object Literal 78

What Values Can You Use?..79

Using it as part of a Function 79

7.2 Accessing Object Properties: Dot Notation and Bracket Notation – Peeking Inside.......................79

Dot Notation: The Simple and Common Approach 80

Bracket Notation: The Versatile Option..81

So, Which One Should You Use?..81

7.3 Adding and Modifying Properties: Dynamic Objects – Reshaping Reality with Code 82

Understanding Dynamic Objects 82

Adding New Properties 82

Modifying Existing Properties 83

7.4 Object Methods: Functions Within Objects – Giving Your Objects Behavior.......................84

Defining Methods: Adding Actions to Objects...84

Calling Methods: Putting Objects to Work 85

Using "this" to work with objects 85

7.5 The this Keyword: Referring to the Current Object – Understanding Context 86

Conclusion: Modeling the Real World 87

Chapter 8: Introduction to Asynchronous JavaScript: Making the Web Responsive – Beyond the Sequential World 88

8.1 Understanding Asynchronous Programming – Keeping Your Webpage Alive! 88

Loading Websites: An Example 88

8.2 Callbacks: Handling Asynchronous Operations – The Old Way to Handle Non-Blocking Operations 89

Deconstructing the Callbacks 90

Cleaning the mess with Callbacks 91

Limitations 92

8.3 Promises: A Better Way to Manage Asynchronous Code – A Promise of Results 92

8.4 async and await: Simplifying Asynchronous Code – Making Asynchronous Code Readable 93

Async 94

Await 94

Why All This Is Important 95

8.5 Fetch API: Making Network Requests – Talking to the Server 95

Conclusion: Responding to the Pace of Today's Web 96

Chapter 9: Enhancing Web Pages with Libraries: jQuery and Beyond (Overview) – Standing on the Shoulders of Giants 97

9.1 What are JavaScript Libraries? – Expanding Your Coding Arsenal 97

9.2 Introduction to jQuery: Simplifying DOM Manipulation – The Classic Library 98

9.3 Other Popular Libraries: React, Angular, Vue (Brief Overview) – The Powerhouses of Modern Web Development 100

1. React: The Component-Based Powerhouse 100

2. Angular: The Comprehensive Framework 101

3. Vue: The Progressive Framework 101

9.4 When to Use a Library (and When Not To) – Making the Right Choice 101

Conclusion: An Overview of Libraries 102

Chapter 10: Putting It All Together: Mini-Projects – Unleashing Your Creativity 103

10.1 Project 1: Interactive Image Gallery – Bringing Images to Life 103

10.2 Project 2: Simple Quiz Application – Testing Knowledge 105

10.3 Project 3: Basic To-Do List – Task Management 108

10.4 Project 4: Dynamic Content Slider – Captivating Visuals 110

10.5 Project 5: Interactive Form with Validation – Refined Data Input.............................112

Conclusion: A New Journey..115

Conclusion: Next Steps – Your Web Development Adventure Awaits!....................................116

Key Takeaways and Next Steps – Building upon Your Foundation.....................................116

Resources for Further Learning – The Tools for Continued Growth...................................117

The Future of JavaScript – A Dynamic Landscape...117

Appendix A: JavaScript Syntax Cheat Sheet...117

Appendix B: Setting Up Your Development Environment (VS Code, etc.)..............................118

Glossary of JavaScript Terms 118

Introduction: Welcome to the World of JavaScript – The Soul of the Web!

So, you want to learn JavaScript? Excellent choice! You're about to embark on a journey into one of the most essential and versatile languages of the web. JavaScript is the engine that drives interactivity, brings web pages to life, and powers countless modern web applications. This book is your passport to understanding and mastering this incredible technology.

Think of HTML as the structure of a house, CSS as its design and decor, and JavaScript as the electrical system – it's what makes everything *work*! Without JavaScript, websites would be static and lifeless. But with JavaScript, you can create dynamic, engaging, and interactive experiences for your users.

What is JavaScript and Why is it Essential? – Beyond Static Pages

JavaScript is a scripting language that runs in web browsers (and increasingly, on servers and other platforms too). It's what allows you to:

- **Add Interactivity:** Make your web pages respond to user actions (clicks, hovers, form submissions, etc.).
- **Manipulate the DOM:** Dynamically change the content and structure of your web pages without requiring a full page reload.
- **Create Animations and Effects:** Bring your web pages to life with visual effects and animations.
- **Validate Forms:** Ensure that users enter correct data before submitting forms.
- **Make Asynchronous Requests:** Fetch data from servers in the background, without interrupting the user experience.
- **Build Web Applications:** Create sophisticated web applications that rival the functionality of desktop applications.

Simply put, JavaScript is what takes a web page from being a static document to an interactive application. It allows you to create a rich, engaging user experience that keeps visitors coming back for more.

JavaScript's Role in Web Development: The Dynamic Layer

In the classic web development stack (HTML, CSS, JavaScript), JavaScript provides the dynamic behavior and interactivity that complements HTML's structure and CSS's styling.

- **HTML (HyperText Markup Language):** Provides the structure and content of the web page.
- **CSS (Cascading Style Sheets):** Controls the visual presentation of the web page (layout, colors, fonts, etc.).
- **JavaScript:** Adds interactivity, dynamic behavior, and application logic to the web page.

While HTML and CSS define what the user *sees*, JavaScript determines what the user *can do* on the page.

A Personal Insight: When I first started learning web development, I was amazed by the power of JavaScript. It allowed me to transform static HTML pages into dynamic and engaging experiences. It was like giving my websites a brain!

How This Book Will Help You: Visuals, Clear Code, and Practical Projects

This book is designed to guide you from zero JavaScript knowledge to writing your own interactive web pages with confidence. Here's how we'll achieve that:

- **Visual Learning:** We'll use diagrams, illustrations, and screenshots to explain complex concepts visually. Because let's face it, Javascript can get complex!
- **Clear, Concise Code Examples:** We'll provide plenty of well-commented code examples that you can copy, paste, and modify.
- **Step-by-Step Instructions:** We'll break down complex tasks into smaller, more manageable steps.
- **Beginner-Friendly Approach:** We'll avoid jargon and explain everything in plain English.
- **Focus on Practical Skills:** We'll focus on the skills you need to build real-world web pages.
- **Engaging Mini-Projects:** At the end of the book, you'll put your skills to the test by building a series of fun and engaging mini-projects.

This book is designed to be accessible and engaging for beginners. We believe that anyone can learn JavaScript with the right guidance and the right resources.

Setting Up Your Development Environment: Your Coding Workshop

Before we can start writing JavaScript code, you'll need to set up your development environment. Don't worry, it's easier than you might think! You'll need two things:

1. **A Text Editor:** This is where you'll write your JavaScript code. We recommend using VS Code (Visual Studio Code), a free, open-source, and highly customizable text editor that is popular among web developers. However, any text editor will do!
2. **A Web Browser:** This is where you'll run your JavaScript code. Any modern web browser (Chrome, Firefox, Safari, Edge) will work.

In Appendix B, we'll provide detailed, step-by-step instructions for setting up your development environment.

Now, let's take this leap into this adventure together. The next steps will allow you to use JS!

Chapter 1: JavaScript Fundamentals: Your First Steps – Laying the Groundwork

Welcome to Chapter 1! We're jumping right in and getting our hands dirty with JavaScript code. In this chapter, you'll learn the fundamental concepts that form the foundation of all JavaScript programs. Think of this as learning the basic chords on a guitar before you start playing songs.

We'll write your first JavaScript code (the classic "Hello, World!"), understand how to include JavaScript in your HTML pages, learn how to use the console for debugging, explore variables for storing data, and discover the core data types that JavaScript uses. Let's begin!

1.1 Writing Your First JavaScript Code: "Hello, World!" – Teaching the Web to Talk

The "Hello, World!" program is a cornerstone of programming. It's the first step, like tuning an instrument before a concert or prepping your brushes before painting. This code is a test to ensure everything is set up correctly.

At its core, the "Hello, World!" program displays the phrase "Hello, World!" to your screen. It's a milestone that shows your environment is able to execute code. The simplicity of accomplishing this task is a testament to the power of Javascript.

The Code Itself

The "Hello, World!" program in Javascript is one line:

```
alert("Hello, World!");
```

That's really it! That's all that's needed to display a message to the user using Javascript. We can break this line down.

- `alert()`
  This is a pre-built function. It's a self-contained program that you can activate, similar to using tools in a toolbox. We use the parentheses to indicate that we want to activate this function.
- `"Hello, World!"`
  This is a string. The quotations around "Hello, World!" are essential to tell the interpreter that this is a string. Otherwise, the interpreter would try to run it as a command.

This code is simple. It can be copied, pasted, and modified.

A Personal Insight: I know that you see that line and say "that's it?" or think it's too easy. But it's essential that you can get that code running. It's easy to dismiss as trivial, but the next steps will be that much easier.

Putting It into Action

Here are the steps to get that line of code running.

1. **Open a Text Editor:** Any text editor will do. Or, you can use VS Code (which is recommended).
2. **Make an HTML File:** Enter the following code into the text editor.

```
<!DOCTYPE html>
<html>
<head>
    <title>JavaScript is Alive</title>
</head>
<body>
    <p>Welcome</p>
    <script>
        alert("Hello, World!");
    </script>
</body>
</html>
```

- **What this HTML does:**
  - `<!DOCTYPE html>`
    This line tells your machine that this is HTML5 code. It should be included to let your browser properly render your document.
  - `<html></html>`
    HTML files have an open and closing html tag.
  - `<head></head>`
    This head tag includes information such as the title.
  - `<body></body>`
    All visible material is put inside the body tags.
  - `<script>alert("Hello, World!");</script>`
    This set of tags allow you to execute Javascript code in your document. It opens and closes with the appropriate tags.

1. **Save the file:** This is crucial! Save the file with a `.html` extension. The `.html` extension tells your computer that this is a HTML file. It can be named "index.html".
2. **Open in your Browser:** Now, open the document in your Browser. If a popup shows up, you've done it correctly!

Troubleshooting

If you do not see the popup, this is what you should look for:

- *Typos*: Javascript doesn't handle typos well. Make sure every bracket has a match!
- *File Extension*: Did you save the file with the `.html` extension?
- *Javascript Enabled:* Is Javascript enabled? This is the most common issue!

A Personal Insight: It was hard to figure out why a seemingly easy problem had occurred when I first started programming. It can be frustrating, but being methodical is key!

Why Is This Important?

Confirming that your environment is working is critical to the coding experience. This allows you to experiment, iterate, and learn Javascript!

1.2 Understanding the <script> Tag: Inline vs. External Scripts – Connecting JavaScript to HTML

Now that you have your JavaScript code, you need to include it in your HTML page. There are two main ways to do this: inline scripts and external scripts.

- **Inline Scripts:** You can embed JavaScript code directly into your HTML page using the <script> tag. The <script> tag tells the browser that the code between the opening and closing tags is JavaScript code that should be executed.
- <!DOCTYPE html>
- <html>
- <head>
-   <title>My First JavaScript Page</title>
- </head>
- <body>
-   <h1>Hello, World!</h1>
-   <script>
-     alert("Hello, World!");
-   </script>
- </body>
  </html>

In this example, the <script> tag is placed at the end of the <body> element. This is a common practice because it ensures that the HTML elements have loaded before the

JavaScript code tries to manipulate them.
The alert pops up when the page is loaded!

- **External Scripts:** You can also store JavaScript code in a separate file (with a .js extension) and then link to that file from your HTML page using the <script> tag with the src attribute.

  1. Create a file called script.js and paste the JavaScript code into it:
  2. // script.js
     alert("Hello, World!");

  3. Link to the script.js file from your HTML page:
  4. <!DOCTYPE html>
  5. <html>
  6. <head>
  7.   <title>My First JavaScript Page</title>
  8. </head>
  9. <body>
  10.   <h1>Hello, World!</h1>
  11.   <script src="script.js"></script>
  12. </body>
      </html>

- In this example, the src attribute tells the browser to load the JavaScript code from the script.js file. Make sure the script.js file is in the same directory as your HTML file.
- **Inline vs. External Scripts: Which is Better?**
  - **Inline Scripts:** Are convenient for small snippets of code or for code that is specific to a single page.
  - **External Scripts:** Are better for larger amounts of code, as they promote code reuse, improve organization, and make it easier to maintain your code.

It's better practice to have most JS code in an external file!

A Personal Insight: I generally prefer to use external scripts, as it helps to keep my HTML and JavaScript code separate and makes it easier to manage my projects.

1.3 Working with the Console: Debugging and Output – Your Secret Weapon for Web Development

So, you've started writing some Javascript, which means you're going to run into problems sooner or later. That's normal! Programming requires the ability to problem solve, and if you can't identify the problems, there's no way you can implement a solution.

Enter the Javascript console. This is an essential tool for debugging. With it, you can see any errors, evaluate variables at different stages, and really know how your code is executing.

Accessing the Javascript Console

Fortunately, the Javascript console is just a button press away.

For most Browsers, you can use:

- Ctrl + Shift + J (Windows)
- Cmd + Option + J (MacOS)

Alternatively, you can search for "Inspect Element" which will open up a series of tools for web design, including the console. If you aren't seeing the same thing as your neighbor, it might be because you have different browser! In general, Chrome and Firefox have the best developer tools for web development.

A Personal Insight: I find that I typically only use the keyboard command, as it's just that much more efficient!

Using the Console - The Key Functions

- **console.log()**

Of all console commands, you will probably use this one the most! It's used to display general information or the values of variables.

```
let name = "Alice";
console.log("The user's name is", name) // The user's name is Alice
```

- **console.warn()**

Use this one to indicate warnings. It will format the message with a different color!

```
if (password.length < 8) {
  console.warn("Password too short");
}
```

- **console.error()**

Use this one to indicate an error. You'll usually find these messages when your program breaks and needs to be debugged.

```
if (age < 0) {
  console.error("The age is invalid");
}
```
  - **console.table()**

Use this one to display structured data.

```
const studentInfo = {
    name: "Alice",
    age: 20,
    major: "Computer Science"
};
console.table(studentInfo)
/*
(index) Value
age      20
major    "Computer Science"
name     "Alice"
*/
```

Using these commands allows you to really see what's going on "under the hood."

A Personal Insight: I have used the console commands so many times. Once, my code wasn't working, even after many fixes. Using the console, I printed out the code line by line. After doing so, I finally found out what my code was doing (and that it was not at all what I had meant!)

Why Is This Important?

The javascript console will help you avoid frustration in your coding projects. It helps with both development and identifying problems. If you don't know how to use it, you would only be shooting in the dark.

Here are some additional tips when using the Javascript console:

  - Learn about different error messages. There are a wide variety of them, but after some experience you will start seeing the same messages and quickly understand how to solve them.
  - Utilize debugging tools in Chrome's sources panel. Javascript has additional tools beyond just the console. You can use the sources to implement break points, watch certain variables, and step into function calls.

With these commands in place, you now have a very valuable tool for both debugging and development.

1.4 Variables: Storing Data with Names – Giving Your Code a Memory

You now know how to output data to a console. Well, that data might come from *variables*, which allow you to assign names to different pieces of data. Think of variables as convenient containers to store various bits of information. Just like variables in math allow you to create powerful equations, variables in code provide the backbone for powerful scripts.

In this section, we'll explore how to declare variables, assign values to them, and follow best practices for naming variables. This skill is fundamental to all coding and will allow you to create increasingly complicated programs.

Declaring Variables: let, const, and the Historical var

JavaScript offers three keywords for declaring variables: let, const, and var. While var was the original keyword, let and const were introduced in ES6 (ECMAScript 2015) and offer several advantages, including better scope management and reduced risk of errors. It's now considered good practice to avoid using var and to stick with let and const.

- **let**: The let keyword declares a *block-scoped* variable. This means that the variable is only accessible within the block of code in which it is defined (e.g., inside an if statement or a for loop). You can reassign a value to a let variable.
- ```
  let message = "Hello, world!";
  ```
- ```
  console.log(message);   // Output: Hello, world!
  ```
-
- ```
  message = "Goodbye, world!"; // Reassign the variable
  console.log(message);   // Output: Goodbye, world!
  ```

- **const**: The const keyword declares a *block-scoped* variable that cannot be reassigned after it is initialized. This is useful for constants or values that should not change during the execution of your program. It also forces you to initialize the variable immediately on declaration, preventing accidental uninitialized variables.
- ```
  const PI = 3.14159;
  ```
- ```
  console.log(PI);   // Output: 3.14159
  ```
-
  ```
  //PI = 3.14;   // This will cause an error (cannot reassign a const
  variable)
  ```
  ```

- **var (Historical):** The var keyword declares a function-scoped or globally-scoped variable, depending on where it is declared. Variables declared with var are accessible throughout the entire function (if declared inside a function) or throughout the entire program (if declared outside of any function).

Because of the risk, it is strongly advised that you avoid the keyword var.

```
function example() {
  if (true) {
    var x = 10; // var is not block-scoped so it's still available
  }
  console.log(x); // Output: 10
}
example()
```

A Personal Insight: I almost exclusively use let and const in my JavaScript code. They provide better scope management and help me to avoid common errors. I only use var when I'm working with older code that hasn't been updated to use ES6.

Variable Naming Conventions: Readability Matters

Choosing good variable names is essential for writing code that is easy to understand and maintain. While Javascript gives you a fair amount of freedom in naming variables, there are some rules and guidelines that you should follow:

1. **Begin with a Letter, Underscore, or Dollar Sign:** Variable names must start with either a letter (a-z, A-Z), an underscore (_), or a dollar sign ($). Starting with a number is not allowed.
2. **Letters, Numbers, Underscores, and Dollar Signs Only:** After the first character, variable names can contain letters, numbers, underscores, and dollar signs. Special characters like hyphens, spaces, or punctuation marks are not allowed.
3. **Case Sensitivity:** JavaScript is case-sensitive, so myVariable is different from myvariable.
4. **Avoid Reserved Keywords:** You cannot use JavaScript reserved keywords (also called reserved words) as variable names. Keywords are words that have special meaning in JavaScript, such as if, else, for, while, function, return, etc.

Follow these conventions to write cleaner Javascript:

1. **Descriptive Names:** Choose names that clearly indicate the purpose of the variable. numberOfStudents is much better than nos.
2. **Camel Case:** Use camel case (lowercase letters for the first word and uppercase letters for subsequent words). For example: userName, productPrice, totalAmount.

3. **Be Brief:** While descriptive names are important, avoid excessively long names. Use abbreviations sparingly and only when they are widely understood.

```javascript
// Good variable names
let studentName = "Alice";
const productPrice = 9.99;
let numberOfItems = 10;
let isActive = true;


// Bad variable names
let x = 10;   // (Too vague)
let p = 9.99; // (Unclear meaning)
let nos = 10; // (Cryptic abbreviation)
//let 1stItem = "Book"; // (Invalid - starts with a number)
```

Assigning Values: Putting Data into Your Containers

Once you've declared a variable, you need to assign a value to it. This is done using the assignment operator (=). The value on the right side of the assignment operator is assigned to the variable on the left side.

```javascript
let age = 30;
let name = "Bob";
const isStudent = true;
```

You can also declare and initialize a variable in the same line:

```javascript
let age = 30;   // Declaration and initialization in one line
```

A Personal Insight: When I first started learning JavaScript, I was confused by the distinction between declaration and assignment. I thought that they were the same thing. But I quickly learned that they are separate operations, and that understanding the difference is important for writing correct code.

With just these skills, you are able to use Javascript as an effective calculator or data manager!

1.5 Data Types: Numbers, Strings, Booleans – Classifying the Information Your Code Handles

You've learned how to create variables to store information, but what *kind* of information can you store? That's where data types come in. Think of data types as labels that classify the different kinds of values your variables can hold. Knowing which data type to use for a certain type of data helps Javascript execute code correctly.

We'll explore the three most fundamental data types in JavaScript: Numbers, Strings, and Booleans. These are the building blocks for representing and manipulating data in your programs.

Numbers: Representing the Quantitative World

The Number data type is used to represent numeric values in JavaScript. Numbers can be integers (whole numbers) or floating-point numbers (numbers with a decimal point).

Unlike some other programming languages, JavaScript doesn't have separate types for integers and floats. All numbers are represented as double-precision 64-bit floating-point values (IEEE 754 standard).

```
let age = 30;              // Integer
let price = 9.99;          // Floating-point number
let temperature = -10.5; // Negative number
```

You can perform various arithmetic operations on numbers using the arithmetic operators we discussed earlier (+, -, *, /, %, **).

```
let x = 10;
let y = 5;

console.log(x + y);    // Output: 15 (addition)
console.log(x - y);    // Output: 5 (subtraction)
console.log(x * y);    // Output: 50 (multiplication)
console.log(x / y);    // Output: 2 (division)
console.log(x % y);    // Output: 0 (modulo)
console.log(x ** y);   // Output: 100000 (exponentiation)
```

JavaScript also provides a built-in `Math` object that contains a variety of mathematical functions and constants.

```
console.log(Math.PI);       // Output: 3.141592653589793
console.log(Math.sqrt(16));   // Output: 4 (square root)
console.log(Math.round(4.7)); // Output: 5 (rounds to the nearest integer)
console.log(Math.floor(4.7)); // Output: 4 (rounds down to the nearest integer)
console.log(Math.ceil(4.2));  // Output: 5 (rounds up to the nearest integer)
```

A Personal Insight: I've learned to be careful when performing arithmetic operations with floating-point numbers, as they can sometimes result in unexpected rounding errors due to the way floats are stored in computer memory.

Strings: Representing Textual Data

The String data type is used to represent text in JavaScript. Strings are sequences of characters enclosed in either single quotes ('...') or double quotes ("..."). JavaScript doesn't differentiate between characters and strings.

```
let name = "Alice";
let message = 'Hello, world!';
```

You can perform various operations on strings using the string methods provided by JavaScript.

- **Concatenation:** You can combine two or more strings using the + operator.
- ```
  let firstName = "Alice";
  ```
- ```
  let lastName = "Smith";
  ```
- ```
  let fullName = firstName + " " + lastName;
  console.log(fullName);   // Output: Alice Smith
  ```

- **Length:** The `length` property returns the number of characters in a string.
- ```
  let message = "Hello, world!";
  console.log(message.length);   // Output: 13
  ```

- **Indexing:** You can access individual characters in a string using indexing. String indices start at 0.
- ```
  let message = "Hello";
  ```
- ```
  console.log(message[0]);   // Output: H
  console.log(message[4]);   // Output: o
  ```

- **String Methods:** JavaScript provides many built-in methods for manipulating strings, such as `toUpperCase()`, `toLowerCase()`, `substring()`, `replace()`, and `trim()`.

- ```
  let message = "  Hello, world!  ";
  ```

- ```
  console.log(message.toUpperCase());          // Output:   HELLO,
  WORLD!
  ```
- ```
  console.log(message.toLowerCase());          // Output:   hello,
  world!
  ```
- ```
  console.log(message.trim());                 // Output: Hello, world!
  ```

```
console.log(message.replace("world", "JavaScript"));  // Output:
Hello, JavaScript!
```

A Personal Insight: Strings are incredibly versatile. I've used them for everything from simple text manipulation to complex data parsing. Mastering string operations is a key skill for any JavaScript programmer.

Booleans: Representing Truth and Falsehood

The Boolean data type is used to represent logical values. Booleans can have only two values: `true` or `false` (note the lowercase). They are used to control the flow of execution in your code, allowing you to make decisions based on whether a condition is true or false.

```
let isStudent = true;
let isAdult = false;
```

Booleans are often used in conditional statements (like `if` statements) to control the flow of execution:

```
let age = 20;
if (age >= 18) {
  console.log("You are an adult.");
} else {
  console.log("You are a minor.");
}
```

You can also use logical operators (`&&`, `||`, `!`) to combine Boolean values and create more complex conditions:

```
let isStudent = true;
let hasDiscount = false;

if (isStudent && hasDiscount) {
  console.log("Eligible for student discount");
} else if (isStudent || hasDiscount) {
  console.log("Eligible for some discount");
} else {
  console.log("No discount");
}
```

A Personal Insight: Booleans are the foundation of decision-making in programming. By mastering the concepts of Boolean values and logical operators, you'll be well-equipped to write code that can adapt to different situations and respond intelligently to user input.

Conclusion: Data, Organized

You've now explored the three most fundamental data types in JavaScript: numbers, strings, and Booleans. By understanding these data types and how to use them, you'll be well-equipped to represent and manipulate data effectively in your JavaScript programs. With these bulding blocks, you can now bring complexity to your Javascript code.

Chapter 2: Making Your Pages Dynamic: Interacting with the DOM – Controlling the Webpage

Welcome to Chapter 2! You've learned the JavaScript basics. Now, let's unlock the real power of JavaScript: its ability to manipulate the web page itself. This is where you transform static HTML into a dynamic and interactive experience for your users. Think of the DOM as the blueprint of your website and Javascript as the contractor who can build upon or modify that blueprint.

In this chapter, we'll explore the Document Object Model (DOM), which is the key to interacting with HTML elements using JavaScript. You'll learn how to select elements, modify their content, change their styles, and respond to user events. This is where the magic happens!

2.1 What is the DOM? The Document Object Model Explained – Your Code's Eye on the Webpage

You've written Javascript code and you've figured out how to display it on your webpage. But Javascript is only useful if it can manipulate the elements on the page! Well, to do that, it needs a map or a guide. This map is known as the DOM or the Document Object Model. Think of the DOM as a living, breathing map of your webpage that JavaScript can use to navigate, read, and modify the page's content and structure.

At its core, the DOM is a *representation* of your HTML document as a tree-like structure. Each element, attribute, and text node in your HTML becomes a node in this tree. JavaScript can then use the DOM to access and interact with these nodes, changing their content, styles, or even adding and removing elements entirely.

Without the DOM, JavaScript would be powerless to manipulate your webpage. It would be like a painter with no canvas or a sculptor with no clay. So, understanding the DOM is absolutely crucial for any web developer.

The DOM Tree: A Hierarchical View of Your Webpage

Imagine your HTML document as a family tree. At the very top is the document object, which represents the entire HTML document. From the document object, branches extend to other nodes, representing different elements in your HTML. Let's look at an example:

```
<!DOCTYPE html>
<html>
<head>
  <title>My Webpage</title>
</head>
```

```
<body>
  <h1>Welcome to My Webpage</h1>
  <p>This is a paragraph of text.</p>
</body>
</html>
```

The DOM tree for this HTML document would look something like this (in simplified form):

```
- document
  - html
    - head
      - title: "My Webpage"
    - body
      - h1: "Welcome to My Webpage"
      - p: "This is a paragraph of text."
```

Each of these elements can be accessed and changed using Javascript.

A Personal Insight: I remember when I first encountered the DOM, it seemed complex and abstract. But once I started visualizing it as a tree structure, it became much easier to understand. I often draw diagrams of the DOM tree to help me plan how to manipulate a webpage with JavaScript.

Key Concepts of the DOM:

- **Nodes:** Each element, attribute, or text node in the HTML document is represented as a node in the DOM tree. There are different types of nodes, such as element nodes, attribute nodes, and text nodes.
- **Relationships:** The relationships between the nodes in the DOM tree reflect the hierarchy of the HTML document. For example, the body element is the *parent* of the h1 and p elements, and the h1 and p elements are *children* of the body element.
- **Properties and Methods:** Each DOM node has properties and methods that you can use to access and manipulate it. For example, the innerHTML property allows you to get or set the HTML markup contained within an element, and the addEventListener() method allows you to attach event listeners to elements.

Accessing the DOM: JavaScript's Gateway

You use Javascript to tell the webpage how to change and adapt the webpage. To do this, you access the DOM via document or window. You will often see code such as:

```
let newText = "New Text";
document.getElementById("elementID").innerHTML = newText;
```

These are some basic methods used to make these changes. We will cover this in the next section. But the important concept to realize is that you are accessing something tangible, even though you can't see it.

A Personal Insight: I think of the document object as a portal that allows JavaScript to reach into the HTML document and change its content and behavior. It's the starting point for all DOM manipulation in JavaScript.

Why the DOM Matters: Powering Dynamic Webpages

The DOM is what allows JavaScript to make webpages dynamic and interactive. Without the DOM, JavaScript would only be able to perform calculations and manipulate data in the background. It wouldn't be able to change the content, styles, or behavior of the webpage itself.

With the DOM, you can:

- **Update Content Dynamically:** Change the text, images, or other content on a webpage in response to user actions.
- **Modify Styles:** Change the appearance of elements on a webpage, such as their color, font, or size.
- **Add and Remove Elements:** Add new elements to a webpage or remove existing elements.
- **Respond to User Events:** Attach event listeners to elements that trigger specific actions when the user interacts with them.

The DOM empowers JavaScript to create rich, engaging, and responsive web applications that provide a seamless user experience.

NOTE: (The Key to Web Interaction)

Understanding the DOM is the foundation for all dynamic web development with JavaScript. It's the key that unlocks the door to creating interactive and engaging web experiences. Now, with this basic concept in mind, you can move to accessing it and manipulating it.

2.2 Selecting Elements: getElementById, getElementsByClassName, querySelector – Finding the Pieces

Before you can manipulate an HTML element, you need to select it. JavaScript provides several methods for selecting elements in the DOM:

- **getElementById(id):** Selects an element by its id attribute. The id attribute should be unique within the HTML document. This is the fastest and most efficient way to select a single element.

- ```
  <div id="myElement">This is my element.</div>
  ```
- ```
  <script>
  ```
- ```
      let element = document.getElementById("myElement");
  ```
- ```
      console.log(element);   // Output: <div id="myElement">This is my
  element.</div>
  ```
  ```
  </script>
  ```

- **getElementsByClassName(className):** Selects all elements with a specified class name. This method returns an HTMLCollection, which is an array-like object containing all the selected elements.
- ```
  <div class="myClass">Element 1</div>
  ```
- ```
  <div class="myClass">Element 2</div>
  ```
- ```
  <script>
  ```
- ```
      let elements = document.getElementsByClassName("myClass");
  ```
- ```
      console.log(elements);   // Output: HTMLCollection [div.myClass,
  div.myClass]
  ```
- ```
      for (let i = 0; i < elements.length; i++) {
  ```
- ```
          console.log(elements[i]);
  ```
- ```
      }
  ```
  ```
  </script>
  ```

- **querySelector(selector):** Selects the *first* element that matches a specified CSS selector. This method is more versatile than getElementById and getElementsByClassName, as it allows you to use any CSS selector to select elements.
- ```
  <div id="container">
  ```
- ```
      <p class="paragraph">This is a paragraph.</p>
  ```
- ```
  </div>
  ```
- ```
  <script>
  ```
- ```
      let element = document.querySelector("#container .paragraph");
  ```
- ```
      console.log(element);   // Output: <p class="paragraph">This is a
  paragraph.</p>
  ```
  ```
  </script>
  ```

- **querySelectorAll(selector):** Selects *all* elements that match a specified CSS selector. This method returns a NodeList, which is similar to an HTMLCollection.
- ```
  <p class="paragraph">Paragraph 1</p>
  ```
- ```
  <p class="paragraph">Paragraph 2</p>
  ```

```
●   <script>
●       let elements = document.querySelectorAll(".paragraph");
●       console.log(elements);   // Output: NodeList [p.paragraph,
    p.paragraph]
●       for (let i = 0; i < elements.length; i++) {
●           console.log(elements[i]);
●       }
    </script>
```

A Personal Insight: I primarily use querySelector and querySelectorAll because they offer the most flexibility and allow me to use my existing CSS knowledge to select elements.
However, getElementById is still useful for selecting unique elements quickly and efficiently.

2.3 Modifying Element Content: innerHTML, textContent – Changing What the User Sees

Alright, you now know how to get Javascript to grab elements from your code! But so what? In this section, we'll see how to get Javascript to do something useful: actually change what those elements do. This is where the interactivity comes to life! To do this, you will need to change the content.

When it comes to changing the content of an element, Javascript gives us two properties to play with: innerHTML and textContent. They achieve the same goal: but in different ways!

innerHTML: Powerful, but Potentially Perilous

The innerHTML property gets or sets the HTML markup contained within an element. This gives you the ability to add, remove, or replace entire HTML structures with code. It is very powerful, and therefore can be dangerous.

Consider the following example.

```
<!DOCTYPE html>
<html>
<head>
    <title>Javascript</title>
</head>
<body>
    <p id = "paragraph">Here is the text that I am looking to change.</p>
    <button onclick="changeText()">CHANGE TEXT</button>
    <script>
    function changeText() {
```

```
            document.getElementById("paragraph").innerHTML = "<b>New Text!</b>";
    }
    </script>
</body>
</html>
```

When pressing the button, the text will be changed to bold text, and a new HTML element is created.

But here's where you must be careful! Notice how the code above has this phrase?

```
<button onclick="changeText()">CHANGE TEXT</button>
```

That allows a user to change the HTML. Now consider what happens if the user inputs harmful Javascript to be injected on the site. This is known as a cross-site scripting attack. There are many ways to resolve it (such as sanitizing or not using user inputs).

A Personal Insight: The XSS risk associated with innerHTML is a real concern. In my experience, it's always better to err on the side of caution and use textContent whenever possible.

textContent: Safe and Simple Text Replacement

The textContent property gets or sets the text content of an element, without any HTML markup.

Consider the same example, but with textContent

```
<!DOCTYPE html>
<html>
<head>
    <title>Javascript</title>
</head>
<body>
    <p id = "paragraph">Here is the text that I am looking to change.</p>
    <button onclick="changeText()">CHANGE TEXT</button>
    <script>
    function changeText() {
        document.getElementById("paragraph").textContent = "<b>New Text!</b>";
    }
    </script>
</body>
</html>
```

In this example, the HTML is literally injected as a string, and the b tags will not be used to make the text bold. This ensures that there are no risks related to XSS, as the injected text is read plainly as text.

A Personal Insight: In general, unless there is a compelling reason to use innerHTML, I would highly advise using textContent

So, which do I use?

Feature	innerHTML	textContent
Functionality	Parses and renders HTML	Renders pure text
Security	Vulnerable to XSS attacks	Safe from XSS attacks
Performance	Slower due to parsing	Faster, no parsing required
Use Cases	Inserting HTML markup	Inserting plain text
Code Example	element.innerHTML = "\<b\>Bold\</b\>"	element.textContent = "\<b\>Bold\</b\>"
Result in Browser	**Bold**	\<b\>Bold\</b\>

A Final Thought

By using innerHTML and textContent you can make Javascript code that makes all of the changes needed to adapt the page to your specifications! You can also make it react to the world by leveraging these techniques to respond to events!

2.4 Changing Styles: style Property, Adding and Removing Classes – Altering the Appearance

You can change the styles of HTML elements using JavaScript, either by directly manipulating the style property or by adding and removing CSS classes.

- **style Property:** The style property allows you to access and modify the inline styles of an element.
- ```<div id="myElement" style="color: blue;">This is my element.</div>```
- ```<script>```
- ```   let element = document.getElementById("myElement");```
- ```   element.style.color = "red";```
- ```   element.style.fontSize = "20px";```

```
</script>
```

While this is useful for simple style changes, it's generally better to use CSS classes for more complex styling.

- **Adding and Removing Classes:** You can add and remove CSS classes from an element using the classList property.

- ```
  <div id="myElement" class="initialClass">This is my element.</div>
  ```
- ```
  <style>
  ```
- ```
  .newClass {
  ```
- ```
      background-color: yellow;
  ```
- ```
      font-weight: bold;
  ```
- ```
  }
  ```
- ```
  </style>
  ```
- ```
  <script>
  ```
- ```
      let element = document.getElementById("myElement");
  ```
- ```
      element.classList.add("newClass");
  ```
- ```
      // Output: <div id="myElement" class="initialClass newClass">This
  ```
  ```
  is my element.</div>
  ```
- ```
      element.classList.remove("initialClass");
  ```
  ```
  </script>
  ```

A Personal Insight: I always prefer to use CSS classes for styling elements, as it promotes a separation of concerns and makes my code more organized and maintainable. I only use the style property for simple, one-off style changes.

2.5 Responding to Events: addEventListener – Listening and Reacting

Events are actions or occurrences that happen in the browser, such as a user clicking a button, hovering over an element, or submitting a form. You can use JavaScript to respond to these events and trigger specific actions.

The addEventListener() method is the primary way to attach event listeners to HTML elements.

```
element.addEventListener(event, function, useCapture);
```

- **event:** The name of the event to listen for (e.g., "click", "mouseover", "keydown").
- **function:** The function to execute when the event occurs.
- **useCapture (Optional):** A Boolean value that specifies whether the event listener should be executed in the capturing phase (default: false).

Here's an example:

```
<button id="myButton">Click Me!</button>
<script>
    let button = document.getElementById("myButton");
    button.addEventListener("click", function() {
        alert("Button clicked!");
    });
</script>
```

Common Types of Events:

- click: Occurs when an element is clicked.
- mouseover: Occurs when the mouse pointer moves over an element.
- mouseout: Occurs when the mouse pointer moves out of an element.
- keydown: Occurs when a key is pressed down.
- keyup: Occurs when a key is released.
- submit: Occurs when a form is submitted.
- load: Occurs when a page or element has finished loading.

A Personal Insight: Events are the key to creating truly interactive web pages. They allow you to respond to user actions and create dynamic experiences that feel engaging and responsive.

Conclusion: Unlocking the Dynamic Web

You've now learned how to interact with the DOM, select elements, modify their content, change their styles, and respond to user events. You've taken that static blueprint we mentioned in the introduction, and started to use that blueprint to build, create and adapt a living and dynamic project!

Chapter 3: Controlling the Flow: Logic and Loops – Directing the Code's Path

You've learned how to manipulate web pages, but so far, your JavaScript code has executed in a straight line. Now, it's time to learn how to control the *flow* of your code, making it dynamic and responsive to different conditions. Think of this as programming a GPS – deciding which turns to take based on your current location and destination.

In this chapter, we'll explore conditional statements (if, else if, else) for making decisions, comparison operators for evaluating conditions, logical operators for combining conditions, and loops (for and while) for repeating actions. These tools are essential for writing code that can solve complex problems and adapt to different situations.

3.1 Conditional Statements: if, else if, else – Making Decisions

Conditional statements allow your code to execute different blocks of code based on whether a condition is true or false. The basic structure of a conditional statement in JavaScript is:

```
if (condition) {
  // Code to execute if the condition is true
} else if (anotherCondition) {
  // Code to execute if anotherCondition is true
} else {
  // Code to execute if none of the conditions are true
}
```

- **if**: The if statement is the starting point of a conditional statement. It evaluates a condition (which must be a Boolean expression) and executes the code block that follows only if the condition is true.
- **else if**: The else if statement allows you to check multiple conditions in a sequence. It's evaluated only if the previous if or else if conditions are false. You can have multiple else if statements in a conditional statement.
- **else**: The else statement is the catch-all case. It's executed only if none of the previous if or else if conditions are true. You can have at most one else statement in a conditional statement.

Here's a practical example:

```
let age = 20;

if (age >= 18) {
  console.log("You are an adult.");
```

```
} else if (age >= 13) {
  console.log("You are a teenager.");
} else {
  console.log("You are a child.");
}
```

Personal Insight: Conditional statements are the workhorses of decision-making in programming. They allow you to create code that can adapt to different situations and respond intelligently to user input.

3.2 Comparison Operators: ==, !=, >, <, >=, <= – Evaluating Conditions

Comparison operators are used to compare two values and return a Boolean value (true or false) based on the comparison. These operators are essential for creating conditions in if statements and loops.

Here are the common comparison operators in JavaScript:

- == **(Equal to):** Returns true if the two operands are equal, and false otherwise. *Important: This operator performs type coercion, which can lead to unexpected results. It's generally better to use the strict equality operator (===) instead.*

- `let x = 10;`
- `let y = "10";`
- `console.log(x == y);  // Output: true (type coercion)`
  `console.log(x === y); // Output: false (strict equality)`

- != **(Not equal to):** Returns true if the two operands are not equal, and false otherwise. *Important: This operator also performs type coercion. Use the strict inequality operator (!==) instead.*

- `let x = 10;`
- `let y = "10";`
- `console.log(x != y);  // Output: false (type coercion)`
  `console.log(x !== y); // Output: true (strict inequality)`

- > **(Greater than):** Returns true if the left operand is greater than the right operand, and false otherwise.

- `let x = 10;`
- `let y = 5;`
  `console.log(x > y);  // Output: true`

- **< (Less than):** Returns true if the left operand is less than the right operand, and false otherwise.

- ```
  let x = 10;
  ```
- ```
  let y = 5;
  console.log(x < y);   // Output: false
  ```

- **>= (Greater than or equal to):** Returns true if the left operand is greater than or equal to the right operand, and false otherwise.

- ```
  let x = 10;
  ```
- ```
  let y = 10;
  ```
- ```
  console.log(x >= y);   // Output: true
  ```

- ```
  let z = 10;
  ```
- ```
  let w = 5;
  console.log(z >= w);   //Output: true
  ```

- **<= (Less than or equal to):** Returns true if the left operand is less than or equal to the right operand, and false otherwise.

- ```
  let x = 5;
  ```
- ```
  let y = 10;
  ```
- ```
  console.log(x <= y);   // Output: true
  ```
-
- ```
  let z = 10;
  ```
- ```
  let w = 10;
  console.log(z <= w);   //Output: true
  ```

A Personal Insight: The strict equality (===) and strict inequality (!==) operators are your best friends in JavaScript. They avoid the type coercion that can lead to unexpected results with the loose equality (==) and loose inequality (!=) operators.

3.3 Logical Operators: &&, ||, ! – Mastering the Art of Boolean Logic

Alright, you know about making decisions with if statements. But what if you want to check *multiple* conditions at once? For that, we need *logical operators*. They're the key to building complex, nuanced logic in your JavaScript code.

Logical operators are how you combine different true/false values to form more nuanced conditions that you can evaluate. Let's think of our previous GPS example: We want the app to suggest a highway route if there is both low traffic and the highway is open. Let's dive into the three main Javascript commands.

- **&& (Logical AND): "Both Must Be True"**

Think of && as the phrase "and also." The && operator only returns true if *both* of its operands are true. If either operand is false, the entire expression is false.

So, with the GPS example,

```
let highwayOpen = true;
let lowTraffic = true;

if (highwayOpen && lowTraffic) {
  console.log("Take the highway route!");
} else {
  console.log("Find an alternate route.");
}
```

In this code, only if highwayOpen and lowTraffic are both true will the GPS suggest the highway.

- **|| (Logical OR): "At Least One Must Be True"**

The || operator, on the other hand, is true if *either* of its operands is true. It only returns false if *both* operands are false. Think of it as "or at least".

So, let's say you want to go out if there's low prices or great reviews.

```
let lowPrices = true;
let greatReviews = false;

if (lowPrices || greatReviews) {
  console.log("Let's go!");
} else {
  console.log("Not worth it. Stay Home.");
}
```

- **! (Logical NOT): "The Opposite of the Truth"**

Finally, the ! operator is your logic inverter. It takes a single operand and returns the opposite of its truthiness. If the operand is true, ! returns false, and if the operand is false, ! returns true.

Let's use the GPS example again!

```
let isDaytime = true;
```

```
if (!isDaytime) {
  console.log("Use headlights.");
} else {
  console.log("No need for headlights.");
}
```

If isDaytime is false then the prompt will tell you to use headlights, in all other cases, it will tell you there's no need!

A Personal Insight: These operators can take time to get used to! I think of them in the English terms to simplify and make sure the conditions actually apply.

Truthy and Falsy Values

Before I go, Javascript also applies the logic to variables and values that aren't explicitly true or false. This is "Truthy" and "Falsy."

Falsy Values	Truthy Values
false	Any other number (positive or negative)
0 (zero)	"hello" (any non-empty string)
"" (empty string)	[1, 2, 3] (any non-empty array)
null	{ name: "Alice" } (any non-empty object)
undefined	true
NaN (Not a Number)	

This means that you can do this:

```
let name = ""; //falsy

if (!name) {
    console.log("You have not entered a name.")
}

name = "Alice" //truthy
if (name) {
```

```
  console.log("Hello, " + name)
}
```

What you should remember is that if it isn't in the falsy value category, it's true!

A Personal Insight: This may seem like extra complexity that isn't useful. However, I tend to use it often to confirm or double check for edge cases.

With Javascript logical operators, you can now create far more complex and adaptive code. These building blocks can be used in many ways and the more you do, the better you will be at it! Now onto the next challenge!

3.4 Loops: for Loops – Automating Repetitive Tasks

So far, you've learned how to make decisions. Now, let's learn how to repeat actions automatically! It can be really annoying if you have to copy and paste the same line of code, such as for printing out all the numbers from 1 to 10. Loops are a way to make your computer do those boring tasks for you!

In this section, we'll delve into the world of for loops, the perfect tool for repeating a block of code a specific number of times. Think of it as a robotic assistant that can execute instructions tirelessly and efficiently.

The Anatomy of a for Loop: The Three Key Components

The basic structure of a for loop in JavaScript consists of three parts, all contained within the parentheses ():

```
for (initialization; condition; increment) {
  // Code to execute for each iteration
}
```

These three statements work together to create the repeating action. Here's what each component does:

- **Initialization:** This expression is executed *only once* at the very beginning of the loop. It's typically used to declare and initialize a counter variable that will track the progress of the loop.
- **Condition:** This is a Boolean expression that is evaluated *before each iteration* of the loop. If the condition is true, the code block inside the loop will be executed. If the condition is false, the loop will terminate. The first time it evaluates to false, the loop ends.

- **Increment:** This expression is executed *after each iteration* of the loop. It's typically used to update the counter variable. This update is what will eventually make the "condition" evaluate to false.

Following the parentheses, the curly braces indicate what Javascript code to apply on every repetition.

A Simple Example: Counting to Five

Let's break it all down with a simple example:

```
for (let i = 0; i < 5; i++) {
  console.log(i);
}

// Output:
// 0
// 1
// 2
// 3
// 4
```

Let's walk through what the machine actually does:

1. let i = 0; sets the i variable to zero.
2. The conditional i < 5 is evaluated and since this is true, the code continues.
3. console.log(i) is executed.
4. i++ is executed. Now the value of i is 1.
5. The conditional i < 5 is evaluated and since this is true, the code continues.
6. console.log(i) is executed.
7. i++ is executed. Now the value of i is 2.
8. And so on and so on until you get to the line to 4.
9. i++ is executed. Now the value of i is 5.
10. The conditional i < 5 is evaluated and since this is false, the code ends.

A Personal Insight: I tend to use for loops to iterate through and change the properties of different HTML elements, which require knowing which element you're dealing with.

Example: Calculating with a Loop

Now, with the looping, we can create some math and have that automated! Here's an example of the first ten numbers.

```
let value = 1;

for (let i = 2; i <= 10; i++) {
  value = value + i;
  console.log(value);
}
```

A Personal Insight: It's always good practice to start with simple loops and gradually increase the complexity as you gain more experience.

Advanced: continue and break

To add some further levels of sophistication to the code, you can use the commands continue and break. These commands can make the loop stop!

- continue: This will end the iteration and continue with the next.
- break: This will end the entire loop.

Here's an example

```
for (let i = 0; i < 10; i++) {
  if (i % 2 === 0) {
    continue; // Skip even numbers
  }
  console.log("Odd number:", i);
  if (i === 7) {
    break;    // End loop after printing 7
  }
}
```

A Personal Insight: These commands can be very useful, although you should be careful about overusing them and making the code difficult to read.

Why Is This Important?

Loops can greatly accelerate the code and increase the capabilities of any program that you are trying to create. What would you like to explore now?

3.5 Loops: while Loops – Keep Going Until...

You now know the for loop, which is perfect when you want to do something a specific number of times. But what if you want to repeat something until *some condition* becomes true? You have the while loop! Think of the while loop as a helpful, if somewhat stubborn, assistant. It just keeps repeating the task you give it until you tell it to stop.

Let's look at the basic framework.

```
while (condition) {
  // Code to execute as long as the condition is true
}
```

That is a bare bones skeleton for a javascript while loop. It may not seem like much, but that bare bones structure can be used to create great, complex programs. Note that you have to be extremely careful to make sure your code will exit at some point!

- **Condition:** This is a Boolean expression. This expression is tested every time the code is executed. If and only if this expression remains true will the loop run.
- **Code to Execute:** The section between curly braces will contain the code to run during each run of the loop.

An Important First Principle!

Before you go any further, understand that you, the programmer, must manage the condition. That means you have to set up the condition to be true and then you have to change something that will make it false at some point. If you fail to do this, you will make what is called an "infinite loop". This will cause your browser to crash.

To illustrate,

```
let count = 0;

while (count < 5) {
  console.log(count);
  count++;
}
```

```
//Will output 0, 1, 2, 3, 4
```

Let's break it down like before:

1. We set the count variable to 0. This is critical to running our while loop. Without this, it is impossible for the expression to work at all.
2. The while command calls count < 5, which, given that count is 0, evaluates to true!
3. The console.log(count) command is therefore executed.
4. The count++ command then increments the value of the counter.
5. Now, back to while! The process repeats again until count = 5.
6. count < 5 is evaluated and is now false. Then the loop ends!

Note what happens if you *don't* put in the line count++. In this case, the value of count will never be updated and you will keep getting count = 0. The loop will never end!

A Personal Insight: For some reason, it seems like a right of passage for all programmers to get stuck in an infinite loop and have to figure out how to make it all stop!

Let's get more practical!

Now, let's take that example and see how we can use the same ideas for a more practical outcome: Asking for a value!

```
let userInput = "";

while (userInput !== "exit") {
  userInput = prompt("Enter a command (type 'exit' to quit):");
  console.log("You entered: " + userInput);
}

console.log("Exiting program.");
```

In the code, the webpage will keep prompting the user for what to type until the user types exit!

A Personal Insight: I find that I can create amazing features and tools, that can run without someone telling the webpage what to do. It opens up the creativity and possibilities.

The importance of break and continue.

The Javascript commands break and continue are critical for any loop and we'll briefly talk about that now.

- **break**

If there is any reason to stop the loop, you use break. Once this command is reached, there is no going back!

- **continue**

If there is a reason to skip this iteration, you use continue. Once this command is reached, the code goes back to evaluating the conditional expression.

Let's see how they work.

```
let i = 0;

while (i < 10) {
  i++;

  if (i === 3) {
    continue; // Skip printing 3
  }

  if (i === 7) {
    break;    // Exit the loop when i is 7
  }

  console.log(i);
}
```

This is what you'll see!

- 1
- 2
- 4
- 5
- 6

A Personal Insight: Many people find the continue command difficult to work with since they have to consider when a code will not be run!

In Conclusion...

You've learned about this extremely valuable command and now have great new powers with Javascript! But make sure you never forget that the code should always have a possibility to stop! So, onwards and upwards!

Chapter 4: Working with Functions: Reusable Code Blocks – Your Key to Efficiency

You've learned how to control the flow of your code, but now it's time to learn how to organize it. Functions are the fundamental building blocks for creating reusable, modular, and maintainable JavaScript code. Think of functions as your personal toolbox, filled with specialized tools that you can use over and over again.

In this chapter, we'll explore how to define functions using the function keyword, how to pass arguments to functions, how to return values from functions, how to understand scope, and how to use anonymous functions and arrow functions for more concise syntax. Mastering these concepts will dramatically improve your ability to write efficient and well-organized code.

4.1 Defining Functions: The function Keyword – Crafting Your Code's Workhorses

Alright, now that you know about the structure of looping. It's time to organize those structures within a reusable block! That's what functions are! By implementing them, you don't have to repeatedly copy the code, which makes your programs simpler.

Think of functions as named containers for a set of instructions. Once defined, you can "call" that function multiple times, wherever you need that specific task performed. In this way, you're building mini-programs within your main program.

The Basic Structure of a Function

The core command is the function command. It looks like this:

```
function functionName(parameter1, parameter2, ...) {
  // Code to be executed
  return; // Optional return statement
}
```

Let's break down the syntax:

- **function Keyword:** This is the magic word that tells JavaScript you're about to define a function. It's essential for letting the interpreter know that you're creating a reusable block of code.
- **functionName:** This is the name you give to your function. You'll use this name to call the function later. It's important to choose a descriptive name that clearly indicates what the function does. Adhering to camel case, as used for Javascript variables, is preferable.
- **(...) (Parentheses):** The parentheses are where you specify the function's parameters. Parameters are variables that will receive values when the function is called. If the function doesn't need any input, the parentheses are left empty. In the future, it will become much easier to inject dependencies with parameters.
- **{ ... } (Curly Braces):** The curly braces enclose the function body, which contains the JavaScript code that will be executed when the function is called.
- **return (Optional):** This is the keyword used to return a value from the function. The returned value can be of any data type. If a function doesn't have a return statement, it implicitly returns undefined.

A Personal Insight: It may not seem like much, but using good descriptive names is essential to understanding the functions. Use them and future you will thank you for helping prevent debugging!

Let's see an example

In this example, we create a function that welcomes you to the app.

```
function welcome() {
    console.log("Welcome to this Javascript app!");
    console.log("Remember to use it safely!");
}
```

Easy! Now that we have created a function, let's learn how to call them! To call a function, simply type the name:

```
welcome() // Welcome to this Javascript app!
```

Now, let's take it one step further!

Let's say you want to use the function on different users. We would need to pass in the user name! This is where parameters come in:

```
function welcome(userName) {
    console.log("Welcome to this Javascript app, " + userName + "!");
    console.log("Remember to use it safely!");
}
```

```
welcome("Alice") //Welcome to this Javascript app, Alice!
```

It's that simple!

A Personal Insight: I consider setting the correct number of arguments key to getting the correct outputs. It's easy to forget about them, so be sure to include them.

Where to put the functions?

It's good practice to put your function in the <head> tag as part of the script portion. For example,

```html
<!DOCTYPE html>
<html>
<head>
    <title>JS is Cool</title>
    <script>
      function welcome(userName) {
          console.log("Welcome to this Javascript app, " + userName + "!");
          console.log("Remember to use it safely!");
      }
    </script>
</head>
<body>
    <p>Welcome</p>
    <script>
      welcome("Alice") //Welcome to this Javascript app, Alice!
    </script>
</body>
</html>
```

Here, the function was defined in the top portion.

4.2 Function Arguments: Passing Data to Functions – Giving Your Code a Voice

To make those functions adaptable, it's now time to use "arguments". These allow functions to have different functionality without changing code. Think of these as passing values into the function to adapt it for different situations.

Arguments allow you to customize the behavior of a function and provide it with the data it needs to perform its task. By using parameters in functions, you can avoid having to recode a function in different situations.

We are going to cover these topics:

- Parameters: The variables that receive values when the function is called.
- Arguments: The actual values passed to the function when it is called.
- More than one Argument: Functions can accept a multitude of arguments.

Parameters and Arguments: Defining the Terms

It's important to clarify the distinction between *parameters* and *arguments*:

- **Parameters:** These are the variables listed inside the parentheses in the function *definition*. They're like placeholders that indicate what kind of data the function expects to receive.
- **Arguments:** These are the actual values that are passed to the function when you *call* it. Arguments get assigned to the corresponding parameters inside the function.

The example from before should make this clear.

```
function welcome(userName) { //The parameter is userName
    console.log("Welcome to this Javascript app, " + userName + "!");
    console.log("Remember to use it safely!");
}


welcome("Alice") //Welcome to this Javascript app, Alice! "Alice" is the
argument
```

A Personal Insight: When I was first learning about functions, I was always getting "arguments" and "parameters" mixed up. I like to imagine parameters as the empty boxes you're building a function for and arguments are the materials that you put into those boxes.

Functions with No Arguments

Just like functions with arguments, you can make a function with no arguments. For example,

```
function greet() {
    console.log("Hello");
}


greet();
```

A Personal Insight: I tend to use argument-less functions to initialize certain HTML properties or inject some specific information.

```
function add(x, y) {
  return x + y;
}


let sum = add(5, 3);   // Output: 8

function logMessage() {
  console.log("This function takes no arguments.");
}


logMessage() // no arguments
```

A Personal Insight: By passing information into functions you can make functions more modular.

More Than One Argument

Of course, functions can have more than one argument. Consider the function

```
function makeGreeting (salutation, name, punct) {
    return (salutation + ", " + name + punct)
}

console.log(makeGreeting("Hello", "Alice", "!"))
console.log(makeGreeting("Bonjour", "Bob", "."))
console.log(makeGreeting("Greetings", "Carol", "..."))
/*
Hello, Alice!
Bonjour, Bob.
Greetings, Carol...
*/
```

A Personal Insight: In cases where the arguments can be optional, I like using "default arguments", which can really make functions more flexible

4.3 Returning Values: Getting Results from Functions – The Output of Your Code

You now know how to create functions that can take in arguments. The next step is getting an output! Well, to do that, you use the return command. You use the return command to send a value (any Javascript data type) back to the portion of the program where the function was called. It's like the delivery service that brings the results of your function's work back to you.

At its core, functions without return statements are useless! Without returns, it's like having a machine that does the thing, but keeps the result hidden inside. Let's consider why this is:

- If a function does not return any values, what can you do with that function? You can, say, print something to the screen but you can't use the functions in calculations or more complicated functions. By returning values, you ensure that you're doing more than just printing!

Let's dive into this code.

- What is a returned value?
- How to make more efficient returns?
- What happens if you don't return?

The Function

For Javascript code, returns are simple. All you have to do is add a command return! Here are some example functions:

```
function timesTwo(val) {
    return 2 * val
}
```

The code will now, given an input val, multiply it by 2 and then return the number. So

```
timesTwo(10)
```

will return 20. Remember that nothing is outputted unless you display the returned value! That's right, just calculating the output isn't the same thing as getting the Javascript to show it!

A Personal Insight: When I first saw the concept of a return, it took some time to get the concept. I would spend hours getting the values to be calculated correctly, only to forget to have it displayed!

Returning Multiple Values

You can also return multiple values through returning an array! Take this function for example:

```
function getAreaAndPerimeter(x, y) {
    const area = x * y
    const perim = (x + y) * 2
    return [area, perim]
}
```

In this function, we have several commands and the output is an array of two values!

A Personal Insight: When returning multiple values like this, it can be very helpful to also return the variable names to make it that much easier to debug. For example, this is how I would write that code:

```
function getAreaAndPerimeter(x, y) {
    const area = x * y
    const perim = (x + y) * 2
    return {area: area, perim: perim}
}
```

Now you know what the code is, just by reading it!

Without the return Command!

So, what happens if you don't use it? If the function gets to the end of the line, it implicitly returns the undefined expression. To see this:

```
function timesTwo(val) {
    const result = 2 * val
}


console.log(timesTwo(2)) //undefined
```

This, to the interpreter, is the same as saying return undefined. This command will, of course, return undefined! In this case, our goal for this code was not achieved and it would have been necessary to add the return.

A Personal Insight: If there's only one command in the function, it can be a good habit to always return, but make sure it fits the style that you are going for!

In Conclusion

Functions are all about creating an input that is useful and a code that can be used! Understanding returns is essential to being able to craft and execute code and programs. Without it, a function is more limited. With these commands in place, what's next?

4.4 Scope: Local vs. Global Variables – Where Your Variables Can Be Seen

You now know how to craft and return Javascript functions. But how do you control how and where the function can interact with other parts of the code?

You now need to learn about scope. Scope defines the accessibility, or visibility, of variables. In other words, it determines where a variable can be accessed and used in your code. Think of scope as the boundaries that define where a variable "lives" and can be seen. The two primary types of scope in JavaScript are local and global.

This topic helps you control the program.

- So what are local variables?
- What are global variables?
- How can you use them?
- What is block scope?

Let's cover it all!

Local Scope: Inside the Function Walls

A variable declared inside a function has local scope. This means that it is only accessible within that function. Local variables are created when the function is called and destroyed when the function returns.

```
function myFunction() {
  let x = 10; // Declared with let, local scope
  console.log(x); // Output: 10 (x is accessible within the function)
}

myFunction();
//console.log(x);    // This will cause an error (x is not defined outside the function)
```

In this code, the local variable x can only be found in the `myFunction`

A Personal Insight: Some people new to coding may want to make every variable a global variable to make their work more streamlined. But they will quickly realize that a global variable can cause errors.

Global Scope: Visible Everywhere

A variable declared outside of any function has global scope. This means that it is accessible from anywhere in the program, including inside functions.

```
let x = 10; // Declared outside a function, global scope

function myFunction() {
   console.log(x); // Access the global variable x
}


myFunction(); // Output: 10
console.log(x); // Output: 10
```

The global keyword is `window`, such as `window.x`.

While convenient, try to use global variables sparingly! If there are issues with the code, it might be hard to understand where the value came from.

A Personal Insight: I find that understanding scope helps me to write more modular and maintainable code. By carefully controlling the visibility of variables, I can avoid unintended side effects and make my code easier to reason about.

Block Scope:

Block scope variables are limited to their braces, such as for loops or in conditionals. If a variable outside the block is referred to and changed, that variable will be referred to. If a variable in the block is newly created, that variable will not exist outside the block.

```
let x = 5;
if (true) {
    let x = 10;  // The "x" inside the if is a *different* variable than the
global x
    console.log(x) // will output 10
}


console.log(x) //Will output 5
```

```
if (true) {
    y = 10; // the y is a *reference* to a larger scope!
    console.log(y)
}


console.log(y) //Will output 10
```

A Personal Insight: It's useful to use block scoping to protect variables from being accessed and used outside of a particular part of code.

4.5 Anonymous Functions and Arrow Functions: Concise Syntax – Streamlining Your Code

You've seen how to declare regular functions. Let's explore Javascript's two more types of functions! This can lead to more versatile coding. In this section, we'll explore anonymous functions and arrow functions, which offer more concise ways to write functions, especially for callbacks and other short, self-contained operations. These Javascript functions can greatly improve the coding.

The two topics will be:

- Anonymous Functions: Quick and Ready!
- Arrow Functions: =>

Anonymous Functions: Quick and Ready

An anonymous function is a function *without* a name. The "name" may be specified later or called directly.

One of the most common ways to use anonymous functions is as callback functions.

```
setTimeout(function() {
  console.log("This message will appear after 2 seconds");
}, 2000);
```

In this case, the anonymous function is the callback that will run after two seconds!

Another common application is with variable declarations:

```
const greet = function(name) {
  return "Hello, " + name + "!";
};
```

```
console.log(greet("Alice")); // Output: Hello, Alice!
```

With the `const` command we can now use that declaration to reuse that code with a name!

A Personal Insight: The anonymous function is useful for simple tasks, as it keeps code from getting too messy. This also helps keeps the code modular.

Arrow Functions: =>

Arrow functions (`=>`) offer a more concise syntax for writing anonymous functions. While they are not exactly the same as function expressions, their brevity makes them very appealing and extremely useful.

The basic syntax is as follows:

```
(parameter1, parameter2, ...) => {
  // Function body
  return expression; //Optional return
}
```

If the function only has one parameter, you can omit the parentheses:

```
parameter => {
  //Function body
  return expression //Optional return
}
```

And if the function body consists of a single expression, you can omit the curly braces and the `return` keyword:

```
parameter => expression
```

Examples:

```
const add = (a, b) => a + b;
console.log(add(2, 3)); //Output: 5


const square = num => num * num;
console.log(square(4))//Output: 16
```

A Personal Insight: What about `this`? Well, the "this" inside an arrow function is the same as the "this" outside of the function. A "normal function" has its own, while the other commands use the context in which it is defined.

Chapter 5: Interacting with Users: Forms and Events – Listening to the World

You've mastered JavaScript fundamentals and can manipulate the DOM. Now it's time to connect with the outside world via events. In the digital world, think of events as the digital touch of the human hand. In this chapter, we'll explore the crucial concepts of HTML forms and events, which allow you to capture user input and create interactive web pages. The sky is the limit!

You'll learn about HTML forms and how to create them, how to handle form submissions, how to access form values, how to validate form data, and how to work with various types of events. By the end of this chapter, you'll be able to create web pages that respond intelligently to user actions and provide a more engaging user experience.

5.1 Understanding HTML Forms: <form>, <input>, <button> – Gathering Information from Your Users

So, you've learned how to change the output of the pages! Now you have to learn how to make your page *respond*! The gateway to Javascript interactivity is HTML Forms! They're how you get user input! But before you can handle that data with Javascript, you must know the various HTML commands to create those forms!

In this section, we'll explore the core elements of HTML forms: the <form> element, the <input> element, and the <button> element. These are the tools you'll use to build the interface for collecting information from your users.

The Core HTML Commands for this topic:

- <form>
- <input>
- <button>

The Foundation: The <form> Element

The <form> element is the container for all the other form elements. This command will allow the browser to handle the information. It's the key structural element of any form. This section requires these properties:

- **action:** This specifies where the data is sent. You might want to send it to a different page, or to another portion of the Javascript.
- **method:** This specifies how to send the data. The two main options are GET (data is appended to the URL) and POST (data is sent in the request body). The data is often transmitted to another portion of the Javascript to be processed.

Putting it together:

```
<form action="#" method="get">

<!--Input Methods Here-->

</form>
```

A Personal Insight: In this example, it's critical that the action section is correctly done! When creating my first forms, I would often forget this element, and think that my form is broken.

Gathering Information: The <input> Element

This element is what people think about for forms. It's what we use to specify different kinds of inputs. The most important is the "type".

- **type="text"**: A basic text input field for single-line text.
- ```
  <label for="name">Name:</label><br>
  <input type="text" id="name" name="name">
  ```

- **type="password"**: A password input field. The characters are masked for security.
- ```
  <label for="password">Password:</label><br>
  <input type="password" id="password" name="password">
  ```

- **type="email"**: An input field specifically for email addresses, with built-in validation.
- ```
  <label for="email">Email:</label><br>
  <input type="email" id="email" name="email">
  ```

- **type="checkbox"**: A checkbox that allows the user to select one or more options.
- ```
  <input type="checkbox" id="agree" name="agree" value="yes">
  <label for="agree">I agree to the terms and conditions</label>
  ```

- **type="radio"**: Radio buttons that allow the user to select only one option from a group. All radio buttons in a group must have the same name attribute.
- ```
  <input type="radio" id="male" name="gender" value="male">
  ```
- ```
  <label for="male">Male</label><br>
  ```
- ```
  <input type="radio" id="female" name="gender" value="female">
  ```
- ```
  <label for="female">Female</label>
  ```

- **type="number"**: An input field for numeric values, with built-in validation.

- ```
  <label for="age">Age:</label><br>
  <input type="number" id="age" name="age" min="0" max="120">
  ```

- **Attributes for Inputs:** In addition to the type attribute, input elements have several other important attributes. Here are a few:
  - id: A unique identifier for the element, used to access it with JavaScript.
  - name: The name of the input field, used to identify the data when the form is submitted.
  - value: Specifies the initial value of the input field. For radio buttons and checkboxes, it's the value that will be submitted if the option is selected.
  - placeholder: Specifies a hint that describes the expected value of the input field. This text is displayed inside the input field when it is empty.
  - required: Specifies that the input field is required and must be filled out before the form can be submitted.

A Personal Insight: Knowing all of these settings can seem impossible at first. But getting used to them allows you to implement all sorts of features on your webpages!

The Final Link: The <button> Element

While <input type="submit"> has been used to indicate which key will submit the form, to have more options, there is <button>!

It has the type to help the browser know its function:

- **type="submit"**: Submits the form data to the URL specified in the action attribute of the <form> element.
- **type="reset"**: Resets the form, clearing all the input fields to their default values.
- **type="button"**: A generic button that can be used to trigger JavaScript code.

```
<button type = "submit">Submit!</button>
```

This line is what you should add to the form. The text will show up.

A Personal Insight: The flexibility in the different kinds of input mean that you can create any kind of data entry and allow users to interact with your system.

5.2 Handling Form Submission: Preventing Default Behavior – Becoming the Gatekeeper

You've built an HTML form, but what happens when the user clicks that "Submit" button? By default, the browser will refresh and send the data to a specified page. However, that will lose all your
```

coding! Well, to resolve that you have to take control of it. To prevent the default behavior you can then specify, with Javascript, what exactly to do with that information.

In this section, we'll discuss how to prevent the default form submission behavior so that we can work with that data in Javascript.

What will be included:

- Understanding Default Form Submission
- Using the Javascript Code

Understanding Default Form Submission

When a user submits a form, these two things happen:

1. **The page refreshes:** The webpage automatically reloads
2. **Submits the Data to the URL:** The data is encoded and set to the URL you specify.

What you've specified on the HTML portion will matter significantly when understanding what your code is doing.

The Javascript Code

In most scenarios, this is where you'll want to prevent the form's default action. To do this, you'll use the event.preventDefault() method. Here's how it works:

1. **Grab the Form:** First, you use what you learned from chapter two and add an identifier to the document.

```html
<form id="myForm" action="#" method="post">
  <!-- Form elements go here -->
  <button type="submit">Submit</button>
</form>
```

1. **Add a Listener:** You then use this and addEventListener to look out for any user's submission.

```javascript
const form = document.getElementById('myForm');

form.addEventListener('submit', function(event) {
  // your code
});
```

1. **Prevent the Action** To actually make sure nothing happens, use the event.preventDefault command! The event part of the input is automatically passed to this code.

```
const form = document.getElementById('myForm');

form.addEventListener('submit', function(event) {
    event.preventDefault(); //Code to avoid action here!
});
```

A Personal Insight: It's helpful to add this line of code even if you have nothing to put within the function. It'll prevent confusion about why your submit function isn't working!

Here is a full function

To put it all together and see what happens, try it out:

```
<!DOCTYPE html>
<html>
<head>
    <title>JS is cool</title>
</head>
<body>
    <form id = "form" action = "#" method = "get">
        First name: <input type = "text" id = "firstName" value = "Jon"><br>
        Last name: <input type = "text" id = "lastName" value = "Snow"><br>
        <input type = "submit" value = "Submit" id = "button">
    </form>
    <script>
        const form = document.getElementById('form');

        form.addEventListener('submit', function(event) {
            event.preventDefault(); //Code to avoid action here!
            console.log('You just submitted!')
        });
    </script>
</body>
</html>
```

A Personal Insight: When you're first working on forms, try having an empty function with the preventDefault command. That way, you can see your code working step by step!

5.3 Accessing Form Values: Getting User Input – Plucking Data From the Form

With the Submit behavior now handled, you now need to be able to read the data in the HTML form. The real power comes when you can obtain that data and then send it to external APIs or reformat what's on the page.

In this section, we will explore some of the important commands and techniques to make sure that you get all the data you want!

What's Next
Setting Identifiers
Using getElementById to save data
Printing the data back

Setting Identifiers

To read the data, we have to start with adding these to the form elements so we can use the command: document.getElementById("identifier")

```
<form id = "form" action = "#" method = "get">
    First name: <input type = "text" id = "firstName" value = "Jon"><br>
    Last name: <input type = "text" id = "lastName" value = "Snow"><br>
    <input type = "submit" value = "Submit" id = "button">
</form>
```

These elements, such as firstName, will be read to access the values! Note, that the code may be different depending on what you are trying to pull!

A Personal Insight: I have often lost time because I copy and pasted the code, only to find the identifiers are wrong! So double check!

Using getElementById to save data

```
form.addEventListener('submit', function(event) {
    event.preventDefault(); //Code to avoid action here!
    //Get input data
    const firstNameText = document.getElementById('firstName').value;
    const lastNameText = document.getElementById('lastName').value;
    console.log('You just submitted!' + firstNameText + lastNameText)
});
```

The firstNameText and lastNameText is now populated to what was in the HTML forms!

Printing the Data Back

This is pretty simple, but let's create another command that puts the data into a specific element!

```
<p id = "demo">Text here</p>
```

Just add a line of code to populate the value!
Here it is in full

```
<!DOCTYPE html>
<html>
<head>
    <title>JS is cool</title>
</head>
<body>
    <form id = "form" action = "#" method = "get">
        First name: <input type = "text" id = "firstName" value = "Jon"><br>
        Last name: <input type = "text" id = "lastName" value = "Snow"><br>
        <input type = "submit" value = "Submit" id = "button">
    </form>
    <p id = "demo">Text here</p>
    <script>
        const form = document.getElementById('form');

        form.addEventListener('submit', function(event) {
            event.preventDefault(); //Code to avoid action here!
            //Get input data
            const firstNameText = document.getElementById('firstName').value;
            const lastNameText = document.getElementById('lastName').value;
            document.getElementById("demo").innerHTML = firstNameText +
lastNameText
        });
    </script>
</body>
</html>
```

A Personal Insight: One of the most common errors I see occurs when a programmer is trying to reference an HTML object before its actually declared. Just make sure you are calling those variables after the declarations!

5.4 Validating Form Data: Ensuring Correct Input – Protecting the Data

Validating form data is crucial for ensuring that the data submitted by the user is correct and in the expected format. This helps to prevent errors, improve data quality, and protect your application from malicious attacks.

You can use JavaScript to perform client-side validation, which means validating the data in the browser before it's sent to the server. This provides a more responsive user experience, as errors can be detected and corrected immediately.

Here are some common types of form validation:

- **Required Fields:** Ensure that required fields are not empty.

  ```
  <input type="text" id="name" name="name" placeholder="Enter your name" required>
  ```

- **Email Validation:** Ensure that the email address is in a valid format.

  ```
  <input type="email" id="email" name="email" placeholder="Enter your email" required>
  ```

- **Password Validation:** Ensure that the password meets certain criteria (e.g., minimum length, required characters).

  ```
  <input type="password" id="password" name="password" placeholder="Enter your password" required minlength="8">
  ```

- **Custom Validation:** You can also create your own custom validation functions to check for specific conditions.
- ```
  <form id="myForm" action="/submit" method="post">
  ```
- ```
      <label for="age">Age:</label><br>
  ```
- ```
      <input type="number" id="age" name="age" placeholder="Enter your age" required><br><br>
  ```
-
- ```
      <button type="submit">Submit</button>
  ```
- ```
  </form>
  ```
- ```
  <script>
  ```
- ```
      let form = document.getElementById("myForm");
  ```
  ```

```
•
•                form.addEventListener("submit", function(event) {
•                    event.preventDefault();
•                    let age = document.getElementById("age").value;
•                    if(age < 0 || age > 150) {
•                        alert("Age is an invalid value!");
•                    }
•                });
            </script>
```

A Personal Insight: Form validation is a critical security measure. It helps to prevent malicious users from injecting harmful code into your application through form input.

Making a Good Look

Users might not know what you want them to put it! So make sure your data is clear, concise, and helpful! To that extent, there are HTML implementations to indicate what to put. Two such are:

- **Placeholder**: Displays the information directly in the field.
- **Tooltip**: Displays when you hover over the text.

```
First name: <input type = "text" id = "firstName" value = "Jon"
placeholder="Your first name"><br>
    Last name: <input type = "text" id = "lastName" value = "Snow" title =
"Your last name"><br>
```

A Personal Insight: What I recommend is making an input that is "for dummies" - meaning, it guides the user with easy and clear steps to do everything. This increases conversions!

5.5 Working with Events: click, submit, mouseover – Making Pages React!

You now know how to get the data that people are putting in. What then? Javascript is able to listen to inputs and activities of users to run some code! These activities are called *events*. Think of events as opportunities for your JavaScript code to spring into action and make the webpage respond to what the user is doing!

Events are core to web Javascript to build interactive web pages. Here's how you can set them:

How to setup your website to use actions.

The most important command is addEventListener. To use it, you just have to remember some syntax

```
element.addEventListener(event, function)
```

To break it down,

- element is the HTML element
- addEventListener is the command to start looking out for a potential event.
- event is the Javascript name of the HTML event.
- function is the Javascript command that runs.

Let's think of an example:

```html
<!DOCTYPE html>
<html>
<head>
<title>Page Title</title>
</head>
<body>

<button id="myBtn">Click me</button>

<script>
document.getElementById("myBtn").addEventListener("click", function() {
  alert("Hello World!");
});
</script>

</body>
</html>
```

In this case, the button is hooked up to addEventListener which runs the alert popup "Hello World!".

As you've probably noticed, the power here is with what you choose to do in the function!

A Personal Insight: There are many types of events out there, so it may be challenging to understand all the different inputs. As a general rule, if you can do the action, there's probably some event that you can use! Also, it's important to use best practice and put the addEventListener within document.addEventListener('DOMContentLoaded', function(){}); to ensure that all the content has been loaded.

Some Common Event Types

The following sections will break out some of the more common types of event.

- **Click**

This occurs whenever the mouse clicks in the element.

- **mouseover**

This occurs whenever the mouse goes *over* the element.

- **mouseout**

This occurs whenever the mouse goes *out* of the element.

- **keydown**

This occurs whenever the key is down. It is generally tied to a broader document, not a specific HTML element.

- **submit**

This event occurs upon HTML button presses.

A Personal Insight: You can implement a large majority of the types of functionalities with just a few of the events! The code that is implemented is what really matters!

Conclusion: Your Bridge to the User

You've now learned how to create HTML forms, handle form submissions, access form values, validate form data, and respond to various types of events. That means you can communicate with the user and adapt the page to his/her requests. What should we work on next?

Chapter 6: Working with Arrays: Storing Collections of Data – Organizing Information

You've learned about basic data types like numbers, strings, and Booleans. But what happens when you need to store a collection of related data, such as a list of names, a series of temperatures, or a set of product images? That's where *arrays* come in. Think of arrays as ordered lists, perfect for organizing information that belongs together.

In this chapter, we'll explore how to create arrays, access and modify their elements, use various array methods, and iterate over arrays. Mastering these skills is essential for working with data effectively in JavaScript and you will find them essential for everything from making games to presenting large amounts of data.

6.1 Creating Arrays: Different Methods – Assembling Your Collections

You now know what variables are, and you've learned how to connect to and react to web pages. Let's now organize them. If you have a whole bunch of separate values, then you'll want to use Arrays!

In Javascript, Arrays are essential. And learning how to implement, change, and call them are important in making your vision happen.

Well, there's no more delay: Let's explore the different ways to declare and code an array!

Method 1: Using Square Brackets – Easy and Efficient

This is the most popular approach!

```
let myArray = [1, "hello", true];
```

All it takes are these symbols, and the array will be properly created! Javascript is versatile, so the different values can also be a multitude of types, as shown above.

```
let myArray1 = [1, 2, 3, 4, 5]; //Array of Numbers
let myArray2 = ["a", "b", "c"]; //Array of characters
let myArray3 = [1, "b", 3.5]; //Mixed
let myArray4 = []; //Empty Array
```

A Personal Insight: I tend to stick with this method because it's relatively efficient for what I need to do. There's also no need to install any new libraries or understand too much about the functions. All of this makes it easier to use and edit the work I do.

Method 2: The `new Array()` Constructor (Less Common)

The `new Array()` constructor is another way to create arrays. Although, I would recommend that you follow the first command.

```
let myArray = new Array(1, 2, 3, "test");

console.log(myArray) // (4) [1, 2, 3, 'test']
```

Be mindful when only including one element with the `new Array()` declaration. The value will be the array *size*, not the contents!

```
let myArray = new Array(3);

console.log(myArray) // (3) [empty × 3]
```

A Personal Insight: The other thing about using this that I do not prefer is that you create something that can look similar but have different behaviours depending on the implementation. This is bad practice as someone else looking at your code, even you, may not understand that it's completely different.

6.2 Accessing Array Elements: Indexing – Pointing to the Data You Need

You now know how to create arrays, but what about accessing the information that's stored inside them? That's where indexing comes in. Think of indexing as a street address system for your array, allowing you to pinpoint the exact location of a specific piece of data.

Arrays use index numbers to get the information. These numbers start at 0, not 1! It can be confusing at first but it becomes intuitive after a while.

Let's start with an example:

```
let myArray = ["A", "B", "C", "D", "E"]
```

To get "A", the index that you would call is 0. So

```
myArray[0] //"A"
myArray[1] //"B"
myArray[2] //"C"
myArray[3] //"D"
```

```
myArray[4]  //"E"
```

A Personal Insight: When I first coded these out, my mind would think that the first item should be `myArray[1]` and it took conscious effort to stop doing!

Javascript does this so that it can be easily referenced and more efficient.

Reading the Index

After understanding the basics, you'll have to put it to use. You can use `[]` to implement code.

For example:

```
let myArray = ["A", "B", "C", "D", "E"];

function showFifthElement(arr) {
    return arr[4];
}

console.log(showFifthElement(myArray)) // outputs "E"
```

Here, we take the data from the array and create a useful function that leverages what's in the array.

What to do with a longer list?

Now consider this,

```
let myArray = ["A", "B", "C", "D", "E"];

myArray.length // = 5
```

`length` can be used to access any code. Let's say you don't know how long the list is, but you still want the last letter. Well, this is how you do it

```
let myArray = ["A", "B", "C", "D", "E", "F"];

myArray[myArray.length - 1] // "F"
```

This can be hard coded as well,

```
function lastLetter(arr) {
    return arr[arr.length - 1];
```

```
}
```

```
console.log(lastLetter(myArray)); // outputs "F"
```

A Personal Insight: It can be difficult to test different lengths of arrays, so creating different test conditions can be quite helpful!

Summary of What to Do

It can be tricky to first navigate the different elements and array indices. So, as a refresher, be sure to remember the following:

- Arrays start at index 0.
- The index can also be a mathematical expression to determine the correct element.
- The length of the array is the number of elements.

6.3 Modifying Arrays: Adding, Removing, and Replacing Elements – Reshaping Your Data

You now know how to set up the various building blocks to create Javascript lists. But the question is, what do we do with them? Well, it would be great if we could use code to modify these arrays. This is how to add the dynamic elements to your website.

When working with Arrays, you can use:

1. Addition of Elements
2. Removal of Elements
3. Replacing Elements.

With these skills, you can build fully dynamic interfaces.

Addition of Elements

What's code without the ability to make more items? This topic is all about the different commands that Javascript uses to make more items.

1. Push
   push() inserts something to the *end* of the array. Let's think of the following scenario.

```
let newMonths = ["July", "August", "September"];
newMonths.push("October");
console.log(newMonths);
```

After doing that, the logs will output the following:
["July", "August", "September", "October"]

Pretty easy! Let's go to the next one.

1. Unshift
    What about to the front? Well, you can use another common code called unshift(). It follows very similar syntax:

```
let newMonths = ["July", "August", "September"];
newMonths.unshift("June");
console.log(newMonths);
```

After doing that, the logs will output the following:
["June", "July", "August", "September"]

These are two simple commands that allow you to add items to both ends of the code!

A Personal Insight: It's tempting to always just code everything at the start and never have to add new code. But, in practicality, you will likely need to add elements or inject code due to changing circumstances!

Removal of Elements

But what if we want to get rid of the data? Deleting and cutting out code can often seem like something that will never need to happen! But, just like above, there can be a wide variety of reasons to use this in the code!

1. Pop
    This command removes the *last* value in the array. For example,

```
let newMonths = ["July", "August", "September"];
newMonths.pop();
console.log(newMonths);
```

And it will output this:

["July", "August"]

1. Shift
    Similar to above, this code is used to remove the first element, not the last. For example:

```
let newMonths = ["July", "August", "September"];
newMonths.shift();
console.log(newMonths);
```

And it will output this:

```
["August", "September"]
```

Note that, unlike adding elements, the commands only change one element at a time.

A Personal Insight: In my experience, there tends to be a bias towards putting the newly created variables and data at the end. It feels natural! That's why it takes practice to use unshift or shift - because it often doesn't feel as natural.

Replacing Elements

What if we want to keep the same structure, but implement a variable? Well, you can't remove a whole bunch of elements, so you can just replace an element.

Let's say you want to have the third value become "October". Well, as you know

```
let newMonths = ["July", "August", "September"];
newMonths[2] = "October"

console.log(newMonths)
```

Now you are set! It will be

```
["July", "August", "October"]
```

The only thing to really note here is that you can't assign a variable to a number outside the original bounds! For example,

```
let newMonths = ["July", "August", "September"];
newMonths[4] = "October"

console.log(newMonths)
```

It will print this!

```
["July", "August", "September", undefined, "October"]
```

Do you see that undefined? Be sure to always replace, instead of adding, if that's what you intend to do!

A Personal Insight: I like to make my code clear by only using the "replace element" for exactly one. There are better and more expressive commands such as splice() if you want to change more than one at a time.

6.4 Array Methods: push, pop, shift, unshift, splice – Your Array Manipulation Arsenal

Alright, now we want to take the core ideas of adding and removing elements and we want to do it fast! There are certain techniques that are common to using these array commands. You can then modify a list of code by copy and pasting to create a high variety of things.

These are the commands that you can use:

- push: Add to the end
- pop: Remove from the end
- shift: Remove from the start
- unshift: Add to the start
- splice: the most flexible way to Add, remove, and replace with it (from anywhere)

1. Adding to the End: .push()

This command will push to the end of the list. It has very simple syntax.

```
let newMonths = ["July", "August", "September"];
newMonths.push("October");
console.log(newMonths);
// ->  ["July", "August", "September", "October"]
```

A Personal Insight: It's really great to use with HTML to update the list to have something displayed every time you add to it. There is something very satisfying about using these commands to automate how you are working with this Javascript and HTML code!

2. Removal from the End: .pop()

This command removes the value from the array. Note that this is *different* than setting the value to null.

```
let newMonths = ["July", "August", "September"];
newMonths.pop();
console.log(newMonths);
//-> ["July", "August"]
```

The .pop() command is simple and straightforward.

A Personal Insight: A good use of this command is in making "undo" commands, where you track what someone has done and if they click undo, just call the pop command to remove this function.

3. Adding to the Start: .unshift()

It is, in general, more useful to think about the end, but if you want to put data in the start, try this code!

```
let newMonths = ["July", "August", "September"];
newMonths.unshift("June");
console.log(newMonths);
//-> ["June", "July", "August", "September"]
```

And just like that, you've moved a value to the start! This is key if the order is essential.

A Personal Insight: It does happen rarely that you'd need to put new information to the start, unless the array is tracking some outside source of data, such as a chat or the number of people currently on the site.

4. Removal from the Start: .shift()

You can see it!

```
let newMonths = ["July", "August", "September"];
newMonths.shift();
console.log(newMonths);
//-> ["August", "September"]
```

Similar to .pop() this can be used to take off a data point at a start.

5. The Swiss Army Knife: .splice()

We are now at our last, most powerful tool. You've learned about inserting and removing values from the array. And that is great to know. But what if you want to insert in the middle? Well, there is the general purpose splice() command!

There are a variety of options for splice

```
array.splice(startIndex, deleteCount, item1, item2, ...);
```

- startIndex (required): The index where you want to start making changes.
- deleteCount (optional): The number of elements you want to remove, starting from the startIndex. If you omit this, it removes everything from the startIndex to the end.
- item1, item2, ... (optional): New elements to insert into the array, starting at the startIndex.

And let's show them off

```
let myArr = ["one", "two", "three", "four", "five"];

//Remove two elements starting from index 1
myArr.splice(1, 2)
console.log(myArr) //-> ["one", "four", "five"]

//Adds 2 elements at the index location
let myArr2 = ["one", "two", "three", "four", "five"];

//Add two elements starting from index 1
myArr2.splice(1, 0, "extra1", "extra2")
console.log(myArr2) //-> [ 'one', 'extra1', 'extra2', 'two', 'three', 'four',
'five' ]

//Replace one element starting from index 2
let myArr3 = ["one", "two", "three", "four", "five"];

myArr3.splice(2, 1, "replace1")
console.log(myArr3) //-> [ 'one', 'two', 'replace1', 'four', 'five' ]
```

And there's even more! Javascript is versatile and offers a lot of different techniques.

A Personal Insight: After you learn these methods, you may be tempted to only use splice! It is highly flexible! But it comes at the cost of requiring some forethought into what you're trying to code for.

6.5 Iterating Over Arrays: for Loops, forEach – Visiting Every Item in Your Collection

You now know how to create and modify arrays. The challenge is now how to process all the information. If there are 1000 values, what is the best way to visit each element? In this section, we will cover what the important types of loops are. These loops are how you get to every element.

These loops are what we will be exploring

- for loops
- forEach loops

The classic for loop: This is the loop.

```
let myArray = ["A", "B", "C", "D", "E"];

for (let i = 0; i < myArray.length; i++) {
  console.log(myArray[i]);
}

// OUTPUT
// A
// B
// C
// D
// E
```

With the curly braces, any code that you write inside will be applied.
Let's explore another example:

```
let myArray = [1, 2, 3, 4, 5];

for (let i = 0; i < myArray.length; i++) {
  myArray[i] = myArray[i] * 2; // Double each element
}

console.log(myArray); // Output: [2, 4, 6, 8, 10]
```

With this code, you will change every element.

A Personal Insight: Because of the index values and easy-to-understand way the code executes, it tends to be very versatile for whatever coding you want to do.

A simpler method: forEach loops.

While great, it still involves all those index numbers that might confuse and take up space on the code. The goal is to look through every item, not necessarily knowing the number.

In this case, Javascript gives the handy command: forEach().

```
let myArray = ["A", "B", "C", "D", "E"];

myArray.forEach(function(element) {
   console.log(element);
});

// Output:
// A
// B
// C
// D
// E
```

There are a number of arguments you can put. This helps make it easy to implement code, but also does it in a way that may not require you to track as many variables.

A Personal Insight: In the other example, I wanted to track the index, which is why I opted for that command. However, in a lot of cases, that index is not very valuable. That is when forEach will be better. The point of a great programmer is being able to choose the right tool to implement!

Chapter 7: Working with Objects: Representing Real-World Entities – Modeling the World in Code

You've mastered arrays, which are great for storing collections of ordered data. Now, let's explore a more powerful and flexible data structure: *objects*. Think of objects as representations of real-world entities, like a person, a car, or a product. Objects are the heart of object-oriented programming (OOP), and they allow you to model complex data in a structured and intuitive way.

In this chapter, we'll learn how to create objects using object literals, how to access and modify object properties, how to add methods to objects, and how to use the this keyword to refer to the current object. These concepts are fundamental to understanding how JavaScript works and how to build complex web applications.

7.1 Creating Objects: Object Literals – The Concise Way to Build Your Worlds

So, you've learned about arrays which can list different values. Now you want a structure that can pair those values with a property such as a character's name and stats in a game? Enter Objects!

Objects, like lists, store data. Unlike lists, the data is separated by keys and values. If you've worked with other coding languages, you may know this as a dictionary or hash table! Each of these keys can be used to call the data later!

We'll be covering the use of the most popular technique to create objects: The object Literal! Think of the object literal as the elegant and efficient way to create your own custom data structures with ease.

The Anatomy of an Object Literal

An object literal in Javascript is defined using curly braces {} and consists of key-value pairs.

```
let myObject = {
  key1: "value1",
  key2: 123,
  key3: true
};
```

Key: Value

Each of these is an entry in your object, and you can make them whatever you want!

A Personal Insight: Javascript is a lot like English; there are tons of features! In this case, you might be curious about what kinds of keys can be used or other techniques that you can use. In Javascript, it tends to be a lot simpler!

What Values Can You Use?

Javascript is flexible. The value can be any Javascript type!

```javascript
let Alice = {
  age: 30,
  occupation: "engineer",
  skills: ["Javascript", "Python", "CSS", "HTML"],
  isStudent: false
}
```

You can use this to build some powerful and versatile data structures!

Using it as part of a Function

A good use case is that we can build it into functions that will do the work for us!

```javascript
function createPerson(name, age, city) {
    return {
        name: name,
        age: age,
        city: city
    };
}
let Alice = createPerson("Alice", 30, "New York");
```

By using functions, we can make this code all that more useful and dynamic as well!

A Personal Insight: This is extremely useful for creating objects with different values! Before I used it, I would have to copy and paste in the objects and make tiny modifications. With this kind of function, it can be done in one line!

7.2 Accessing Object Properties: Dot Notation and Bracket Notation – Peeking Inside

So you have your shiny new JavaScript object full of neatly organized data. Great! Now, how do you actually get to that data? Well, there are two main ways to do it, like having two different keys to unlock the same treasure chest: dot notation and bracket notation. Each one has its strengths, and understanding them will make you much more effective at using objects.

In this section, we will compare the two Javascript options and recommend a best option to implement.

- **Dot Notation**
- **Bracket Notation**

Dot Notation: The Simple and Common Approach

Dot notation is generally the cleaner and easier-to-read syntax for accessing object properties.

```
let myObject = {
  name: "Alice",
  age: 30,
  city: "New York"
};


console.log(myObject.name);    // Output: Alice
console.log(myObject.age);     // Output: 30
console.log(myObject.city);    // Output: New York
```

With this set of commands, you are set! There is, however, one caveat. For example, this code will *not* work.

```
let myObject = {
  "first name": "Alice",
  age: 30,
  city: "New York"
};


console.log(myObject.first name);
```

If your object has variables with spaces in it, you can't use dot notation. That is where our next strategy comes in!

A Personal Insight: I tend to use dot notation if I have control over the variables that I am setting. As I have seen with other Javascript projects, when there are multiple people contributing, one will invariably make it harder.

Bracket Notation: The Versatile Option

Bracket notation gives you more flexibility. You can use it to access properties whose names contain spaces or special characters.

Here's how it works:

```
let myObject = {
  "first name": "Alice",
  age: 30,
  city: "New York"
};


console.log(myObject["first name"]);   // Output: Alice
```

You can also use bracket notation to access properties whose names are stored in variables:

```
let myObject = {
  name: "Alice",
  age: 30,
  city: "New York"
};


let propertyName = "age";
console.log(myObject[propertyName]);   // Output: 30
```

A Personal Insight: As you can see, the command is far less intuitive than dot notation. There are reasons to use it, but I tend to use dot notation for clarity! Also, watch out! It is very easy to get confused and think you are indexing, like with arrays.

So, Which One Should You Use?

- **Dot Notation:** Use this when the property name is a valid JavaScript identifier and you want cleaner, more readable code.
- **Bracket Notation:** Use this when the property name contains spaces or special characters, or when the property name is stored in a variable.

In general, dot notation is preferred when you can use it, as it is more concise and easier to read. However, bracket notation is essential when you need to access properties with dynamic names or with names that contain spaces or special characters.

7.3 Adding and Modifying Properties: Dynamic Objects – Reshaping Reality with Code

You now have a foundational Javascript Object set up. It's time to take that static structure and put it into the dynamic realm of Javascript!

In this section, we'll explore how to add new properties, modify existing properties, and even delete properties from your objects, all at runtime.

1. What are Javascript dynamic objects?
2. Using dot notation.
3. Using bracket notation.

Understanding Dynamic Objects

Unlike some other programming languages, objects in JavaScript are inherently *dynamic*. This means that you can change their structure and content at any time, even after they've been created. This flexibility is one of the things that makes JavaScript so powerful.

With it, you can create very adaptive structures that are based on the information that comes in, making it extremely useful for adapting code for future purposes.

Adding New Properties

It's one thing to read and return values, but we can now update them dynamically. Adding new properties to the code can happen simply by pointing the key to a value!

The key can be set up using the already described ways:

Dot Notation
To add a property, you simply point to it with

```
myObject.propertyName = value;
```

Bracket Notation
To use it for bracket Notation,

```
myObject["property Name"] = value;
```

Here it is all together:

```
let player = {
  name: "Mario",
  level: 1,
};


player.power = "Jump"; //Using Dot Notation
player["points"] = 0 // Using Bracket Notation

console.log(player)
//-> {name: 'Mario', level: 1, power: 'Jump', points: 0}
```

Here are some tips to keep in mind when dealing with the different properties

- It is *better* to use dot notation for readability. It can be confusing to future coders if special characters are all of a sudden used.
- You can't make a new name for a key. If there already exists a key, you are just updating that, not adding something new!

A Personal Insight: I often take advantage of dynamic properties to add properties to my objects based on user input or data from an external source. It allows me to create objects that are tailored to the specific needs of my application.

Modifying Existing Properties

You can modify existing properties using the same techniques as adding new properties: dot notation and bracket notation. You simply assign a new value to the existing property.

Let's say we wanted to give Mario a power boost. Well, all you would need to do is this

```
let player = {
  name: "Mario",
  level: 1,
  power: "Jump",
  points: 0
};


player.power = "Super Jump";
console.log(player); //-> Output: {name: 'Mario', level: 1, power: 'Super Jump', points: 0}
```

You see that the `power` entry is updated. If, instead, this command was included `player["power"] = "Super Jump";`, the same result would have occurred.

A Personal Insight: Keep in mind that if you had made it a constant by using `const`, that means you would be unable to modify it!

7.4 Object Methods: Functions Within Objects – Giving Your Objects Behavior

You've now learned how to give an object different properties and now you have to figure out what to do with those objects! Let's say you are creating an interactive game with a hero. You might want that hero to be able to act. Well, to give it those actions, you need methods! Methods are just functions assigned to an object's property.

Think of methods as the actions your objects can perform, the verbs to their nouns. Methods are what brings the data to life!

In this section, we'll explore how to define methods within objects and how to call those methods to perform actions.

Let's dive in!

Defining Methods: Adding Actions to Objects

A method is a function that is associated with an object. You can define a method by assigning a function to an object property. Let's see an example:

```
let person = {
  name: "Alice",
  age: 30,
  greet: function() {
    console.log("Hello, my name is " + this.name);
  }
};
```

This method allows you to add the action of greeting! And you can name that action whatever you want!

A Personal Insight: There are a few steps. First, the method MUST be within the Object you're defining. If not, it's just a function that is used to create the object!

Calling Methods: Putting Objects to Work

Now how can you call that action? To call a method, you use the dot notation, just like accessing any other property:

```
let person = {
  name: "Alice",
  age: 30,
  greet: function() {
    console.log("Hello, my name is " + this.name);
  }
};


person.greet();   // Output: Hello, my name is Alice
```

In this case, `person.greet()` calls the function, and therefore that text prints to the log. Pretty easy!

A Personal Insight: Don't forget the parentheses. Just because it's attached to the object doesn't mean you no longer have to signal to the interpreter that you want that code to *run*.

Using "this" to work with objects

In a function, it may be valuable to make use of the variable. To specify the variable that you've created, use this:

```
let person = {
  name: "Alice",
  age: 30,
  greet: function() {
    console.log("Hello, my name is " + this.name);
    console.log("Also, I am this old " + this.age);
  }
};


person.greet();
// Output: Hello, my name is Alice
// Output: Also, I am this old 30
```

Javascript makes it that much easier to perform whatever action and keep track of its values. It can't be emphasized enough that if you don't know what the variable is, you can always print it out to the log!

A Personal Insight: Javascript also allows you to not make this exact format. But this makes it more readable.

7.5 The this Keyword: Referring to the Current Object – Understanding Context

The this keyword refers to the current object in a method. It allows you to access the object's properties and other methods from within the method itself.

The value of this depends on how the function is called:

- **When a method is called on an object:** this refers to the object itself.
- **When a function is called outside of an object:** In strict mode, this is undefined. Otherwise, it refers to the global object (window in browsers, global in Node.js). This is the reason why it is necessary to use function expressions, instead of arrow functions. Because functions defined using arrow functions do not have their own this. In all cases, this refers to the this of the surrounding context.

```
let person = {
  name: "Alice",
  age: 30,
  greet: function() {
    console.log("Hello, my name is " + this.name); //`this` refers to person
    console.log(this)
  }
};

person.greet();  // Output: Hello, my name is Alice
```

A Personal Insight: Understanding the this keyword is essential for writing code that works correctly in object-oriented JavaScript. It can be a bit confusing at first, but with practice, you'll get a feel for how it works.

Conclusion: Modeling the Real World

By mastering the concepts of creating objects, accessing and modifying properties, adding methods, and understanding the this keyword, you'll be well-equipped to model real-world entities in your JavaScript programs and to build complex and interactive applications. You are now fluent in objects!

Chapter 8: Introduction to Asynchronous JavaScript: Making the Web Responsive – Beyond the Sequential World

You've learned how to write JavaScript code that executes sequentially, one line after another. However, many operations in web development, such as making network requests or handling user input, can take a significant amount of time to complete. If you were to perform these operations synchronously (i.e., waiting for them to complete before continuing), your web page would become unresponsive, freezing the user interface and providing a poor user experience.

That's where *asynchronous programming* comes in. Asynchronous JavaScript allows you to perform long-running operations in the background, without blocking the main thread of execution. This keeps your web page responsive and allows you to provide a smoother and more engaging user experience. Think of it as juggling multiple tasks at once, so your page doesn't freeze up while waiting for one thing to finish.

In this chapter, we'll explore the key concepts of asynchronous programming in JavaScript, including callbacks, Promises, async and await, and the Fetch API. Mastering these concepts is essential for building modern web applications that can handle complex operations without sacrificing responsiveness.

8.1 Understanding Asynchronous Programming – Keeping Your Webpage Alive!

You've learned many of the foundational skills in Javascript, and you are learning how you can have some serious impacts on what is happening on your code. But there is one case where Javascript might fall over: Loading things. By default, if your page takes too long to load some data, you may end up waiting. Or worse, your webpage will crash!

Think of asynchronous Javascript as Javascript's method to doing more than one thing at a time! You will want to learn about this, since, without this knowledge, you may find that your web pages may end up unresponsive to user commands.

How can Javascript be coded to run in a way that can deal with all these requirements?

- Let's show the problem.
- Explain what Javascript offers

Loading Websites: An Example

Let's say you want to load some data to your webpage. Your code might look like this.

```
function loadData() {
  const data = fetchDataFromServer(); // Simulate data fetching
```

```
    // Process the data once it's loaded (THIS LINE WILL ONLY RUN AFTER IT
FINISHES)
    displayData(data);
}
```

Now what if `fetchDataFromServer` takes 10 seconds? Or what if it's broken? Well, the user is going to see a frozen or broken website. To the user, your website is just not working!

To solve this issue, you need asynchronous programming! Async Javascript is the solution to avoid loading. In short, instead of freezing your entire app, the process continues to function and will display the loaded data once it can!

How It Works

The machine will know that this is going to be a process that may take a while, so Javascript will skip it for now and put the rest of the work in its queue. The key to do is to use this properly, so the HTML can make the Javascript code work with `addEventListener` and the user will be none the wiser!

Here's the breakdown:

1. **Initiate the action:** The Javascript program identifies that something must be retrieved.
2. **Add it to the Queu:** The Javascript program is placed in the queue so that it can be handled later.
3. **Continue the Javascript:** For the most part, we continue with our normal Javascript until something occurs where it may affect what we are trying to load or display. At that point, the Javascript program will display that something went wrong.
4. **Display the Data:** The Javascript will be ready to run! We have an element to display, and data to print, and now the website looks normal again.

The important point is that while step 1 is occurring, the website can be used without a freeze.

A Personal Insight: I have definitely had a situation where I've created pages and pages worth of good Javascript code, only to be frustrated that the site wasn't usable! It was only when I fully mastered how to use asynchronous programming that I could finally work around the issue and build things I thought to be not possible before!

8.2 Callbacks: Handling Asynchronous Operations – The Old Way to Handle Non-Blocking Operations

So, what's a callback? The purpose of callbacks is to provide Javascript an element to connect to after the action. This function is "called back" to be executed!

Think of callbacks as a way of telling Javascript what to do *after* an asynchronous operation has finished, making sure it won't do something before the code has run.

What this section will cover
*Breaking down syntax.
*Making the code example more robust.
*Problems with Callbacks
*A Personal Insight

Deconstructing the Callbacks

The essential part of Callbacks has two steps:

1. Set up a function to be the callback,
2. Activate that function to trigger after.

You are now setting it up to fire at some point.

Here's an example.

```javascript
function printHello() {
  console.log("Hello!");
}

setTimeout(printHello, 3000); // Delays the execution of printHello by 3000
milliseconds (3 seconds)

console.log("I'm outputting");
```

content_copydownload

Use code with caution.JavaScript

Take note that the output is

```
I'm outputting
"Hello!"
```

content_copydownload

Use code with caution.

The way this works is:

1. `setTimeout` is a function that sets the function `printHello` to occur after `3000` milliseconds.

2. After the timer has completed, the `printHello` function is run and therefore `"Hello"` is shown.

You also do not need to create a separate function! You can create anonymous functions:

```
setTimeout(function() {
  console.log("Hello!");
}, 3000); // Delays the execution of printHello by 3000 milliseconds (3 seconds)
```

A Personal Insight: Note that we are now talking about two different `function` - a type from way back and this current one!

Cleaning the mess with Callbacks

Often, websites need to call multiple functions that rely on others. There comes a point where, with the basic skills we've discussed, you might run out of space. It ends up being a long series of code, one after another. Callbacks allow us to clean it up, but let's see that it is easier.

```
function firstAction(callback) {
    setTimeout(function(){
        console.log('First action completed');
        callback(); // Execute the callback
    }, 1000);
}

function secondAction() {
    console.log('Second action completed');
}

firstAction(secondAction)
```

If there wasn't a callback, the computer would have just automatically called `secondAction` and there would be no guarantees on when or how that would have come!

A Personal Insight: While useful, callbacks can have a negative effect on the look. If there are too many or the functions depend on one another, it looks too messy!

Limitations

While Javascript callbacks are easy to use, they are harder to organize and understand, when code becomes more complicated. In future topics, we will learn how to get rid of callbacks and replace them.

8.3 Promises: A Better Way to Manage Asynchronous Code – A Promise of Results

Promises are a more modern and structured way to handle asynchronous operations in JavaScript. A Promise represents the eventual completion (or failure) of an asynchronous operation and allows you to chain together multiple asynchronous operations in a more readable and manageable way.

A Promise has three states:

- **Pending:** The initial state, representing that the operation is still in progress.
- **Fulfilled:** The operation completed successfully.
- **Rejected:** The operation failed.

You can create a Promise using the new Promise() constructor:

```
let myPromise = new Promise(function(resolve, reject) {
  // Perform the asynchronous operation here
  setTimeout(function() {
    let success = true; // Simulate success or failure

    if (success) {
      resolve("Operation completed successfully!"); // Resolve the Promise
    } else {
      reject("Operation failed!"); // Reject the Promise
    }
  }, 2000);
});
```

To handle the result of a Promise, you can use the then() and catch() methods:

```
myPromise.then(function(result) {
  console.log("Result: " + result);  // Called if the Promise is resolved
}).catch(function(error) {
  console.error("Error: " + error);  // Called if the Promise is rejected
});
```

You can chain multiple Promises together using the then() method, creating a sequence of asynchronous operations that execute in a predictable order.

```javascript
function doSomethingAsync() {
  return new Promise(resolve => {
    setTimeout(() => {
      resolve("First operation completed!");
    }, 1000);
  });
}


function doSomethingElseAsync(message) {
  return new Promise(resolve => {
    setTimeout(() => {
      resolve(message + " Second operation completed!");
    }, 1000);
  });
}


doSomethingAsync()
  .then(message => doSomethingElseAsync(message))
  .then(finalMessage => console.log("Final result: " + finalMessage));
```

A Personal Insight: Promises revolutionized the way I write asynchronous JavaScript code. They eliminated the complexity of nested callbacks and made my code much easier to read, understand, and maintain.

8.4 async and await: Simplifying Asynchronous Code – Making Asynchronous Code Readable

You now know about Promises! Now you can organize and have a solid flow. However, it may still seem quite messy and there is a cleaner way! What if there was a way to read the code as if it was running all the time! Enter async and await! These commands greatly simplify the javascript so you can read and run the code in simple commands.

In Javascript, async and await will allow for more straightforward execution. Javascript has, with the right training, has the potential to create amazing features.

We'll talk about the use of these features
The benefits it gives you.
When to use these features.

Async

To use, all you have to do is add the word async in front of the declaration.

```
async function myFunction() {
  // Code here
}
```

The main point of async is to signify to the compiler (the program that runs to test your code) that the code you are running may involve a task that needs time! It won't solve any of the issues we talked about before. You also can't have the async command by itself as Javascript can't guess that you want to implement asynchronous commands.

Await

This is where the magic happens! With this, you are telling Javascript to pause while the data hasn't loaded! It waits for a Promise to resolve, making sure the outputted command has the information before continuing!

Let's see how it works in code! First, you need to set up your normal command like previously discussed!

```
function resolveAfter2Seconds(x) {
  return new Promise(resolve => {
    setTimeout(() => {
      resolve(x);
    }, 2000);
  });
}
```

This Javascript code creates the promise for something to occur after two seconds. Let's say you want to call a separate function! All you have to do is add async and await to your code!

```
async function add1(x) {
  const a = await resolveAfter2Seconds(10);
  const b = await resolveAfter2Seconds(20);
  return x + a + b;
}
```

```
add1(10).then(v => {
  console.log(v);   // prints 40 after 4 seconds.
});
```

This will run in approximately four seconds! As both a and b are functions that require loading, that is what makes this code asynchronous.

A Personal Insight: This is one of the most difficult aspects of Javascript for others to remember. Even I sometimes have to check to make sure everything is running correctly!

Why All This Is Important

Here are a few things to consider when to use async and await:

- Cleanliness: This helps make it easier to read your Javascript and can be reused if needed.
- More Options: Without these commands, you may end up having to come up with all kinds of work arounds!

8.5 Fetch API: Making Network Requests – Talking to the Server

The Fetch API provides a modern and powerful way to make network requests in JavaScript. It allows you to fetch data from servers, send data to servers, and perform other types of network operations.

The basic syntax for using the Fetch API is as follows:

```
fetch(url)
  .then(response => response.json()) // Parse the response as JSON
  .then(data => console.log(data))   // Process the data
  .catch(error => console.error("Error:", error));
```

Here's a breakdown of the code:

1. **fetch(url):** This initiates a network request to the specified URL. It returns a Promise that resolves to the Response to that request, whether it is successful or not.
2. **.then(response => response.json()):** This handles the response from the server. If the response is successful, it calls the response.json() method to parse the response body as JSON. This method also returns a Promise that resolves to the parsed JSON data.
3. **.then(data => console.log(data)):** This handles the parsed JSON data. It logs the data to the console.

4. **.catch(error => console.error("Error:", error)):** This handles any errors that occur during the process. It logs the error to the console.

You can also use async and await to simplify the Fetch API code:

```
async function getData() {
  try {
    const response = await fetch(url);
    const data = await response.json();
    console.log(data);
  } catch (error) {
    console.error("Error:", error);
  }
}


getData();
```

A Personal Insight: The Fetch API is a versatile and powerful tool for making network requests in JavaScript. I use it extensively to fetch data from APIs, load images, and perform other types of network operations.

Conclusion: Responding to the Pace of Today's Web

By mastering the concepts of asynchronous programming, callbacks, Promises, async and await, and the Fetch API, you'll be well-equipped to build modern web applications that are responsive, engaging, and able to handle complex operations without sacrificing the user experience. With these skills, you are now more responsive than ever!

Chapter 9: Enhancing Web Pages with Libraries: jQuery and Beyond (Overview) – Standing on the Shoulders of Giants

You've now built a solid foundation in JavaScript, and you're ready to take your skills to the next level by exploring the world of JavaScript libraries. Think of libraries as pre-built sets of code that can save you time and effort by providing ready-made solutions to common web development tasks. Instead of reinventing the wheel, you can leverage the work of other developers to build more complex and sophisticated web applications more quickly.

This chapter will provide you with an overview of JavaScript libraries, starting with a deep dive into jQuery, one of the most popular and influential JavaScript libraries of all time. We'll then briefly introduce other popular libraries like React, Angular, and Vue, and discuss when to use a library (and when not to). This is about to open your eyes to a larger world of functionality.

9.1 What are JavaScript Libraries? – Expanding Your Coding Arsenal

You've mastered the core principles of Javascript but what if you need to do more? For that, you can always create and borrow from pre-made tools to make your code better! If you aren't careful, you can waste time trying to recreate something someone else has done! Javascript libraries are collections of prewritten JS code, making it easier to program and build powerful and effective websites with more efficient Javascript.

Think of Javascript Libraries as tools that offer different ways to handle those tasks that are critical for any developer. By implementing it, it will improve your life.

- So what do they do?
- What can they not do?

That is what we'll discuss in this section.

What do they do?

Think of these benefits as a general rule. The specifics depend on the library being implemented.

A Toolbag for Javascript
What all good programmers should do is follow the concept "Don't reinvent the wheel", meaning reuse code when it's available! These pieces are high quality and saves a lot of time!

Easier To Use
Because the code has already been written, it tends to make the code more readable. Some of these commands can be so incredibly complex that even the smallest project becomes more complicated.

Easier to be Cross Compatible

Different browsers implement different versions, with each supporting different versions. These libraries tend to take account of the differences and make it that much easier to implement the code.

A Personal Insight: These codes save so much time when I am just trying to quickly implement functionality. It's better to make sure what I want is effective, before I decide to write code from the ground up.

So, What Can't Javascript Libraries Do?

Libraries are tools, and like tools, they might not fit every job! So, let's check it out!

Won't teach you basic syntax

Javascript libraries are designed for you to save time or create advanced features, not to teach you Javascript, HTML, or other.

Must be adapted or designed to work with your specific system

It may be challenging to implement code, and the library might be more useful for a smaller number of tasks than you expect.

Unreliable and Difficult to Change

For the same reason, the code is designed for others, not for you. Javascript libraries can also change in their versions, which will mess up your code. This is very difficult to adapt the Javascript and has the potential to change your code significantly.

A Personal Insight: I highly recommend you always remember what the underlying structure and what the raw Javascript means, so if these frameworks and codes are no longer relevant, you can always code from scratch!

9.2 Introduction to jQuery: Simplifying DOM Manipulation – The Classic Library

jQuery is a fast, small, and feature-rich JavaScript library that simplifies HTML DOM manipulation, event handling, animation, and AJAX. It was first released in 2006 and quickly became one of the most popular JavaScript libraries in the world.

While modern JavaScript has evolved, and many of jQuery's features are now available natively, jQuery is still a valuable tool to learn, and understanding its principles can help you to write more efficient and cross-browser compatible code.

- **Key Features of jQuery:**
    - **Simplified DOM Manipulation:** jQuery provides a concise and intuitive syntax for selecting, traversing, and manipulating HTML elements.

- **Event Handling:** jQuery simplifies the process of attaching event listeners to HTML elements.
- **Animations and Effects:** jQuery provides a range of pre-built animations and effects that you can use to enhance the user experience.
- **AJAX:** jQuery simplifies the process of making asynchronous requests to servers.
- **Cross-Browser Compatibility:** jQuery handles the inconsistencies between different web browsers, ensuring that your code works reliably across all platforms.

- **Using jQuery:** To use jQuery in your web page, you need to include the jQuery library from a CDN (Content Delivery Network) or download it and include it locally.

```html
<!DOCTYPE html>
<html>
<head>
    <title>jQuery Example</title>
    <script
src="https://ajax.googleapis.com/ajax/libs/jquery/3.6.0/jquery.min.js">
</script>
    <script>
        $(document).ready(function(){
            $("button").click(function(){
                $("p").hide();
            });
        });
    </script>
</head>
<body>

    <p>This is a paragraph.</p>
    <button>Click me</button>

</body>
</html>
```

Here's a breakdown of the code:

1. `<script src="https://ajax.googleapis.com/ajax/libs/jquery/3.6.0/jquery.min.js"></script>`: This line includes the jQuery library from a CDN.
2. `$(document).ready(function(){ ... });`: This ensures that the jQuery code is executed only after the DOM has fully loaded.

3. `$("button").click(function(){ ... });`: This attaches a click event listener to all `<button>` elements on the page.
4. `$("p").hide();`: This hides all `<p>` elements on the page when the button is clicked.

A Personal Insight: jQuery was a game-changer for me when I first started learning web development. It made DOM manipulation so much easier and allowed me to create complex and interactive web pages with relatively little code.

9.3 Other Popular Libraries: React, Angular, Vue (Brief Overview) – The Powerhouses of Modern Web Development

You've gotten a taste of what a framework does for the Javascript landscape! Well, it's time to take a look at what people are actually using! These three frameworks, React, Angular, and Vue, are used widely in modern frameworks! Instead of a basic look at everything from the building blocks, we will be focusing on the general purpose of what's out there.

The Frameworks

- React
- Angular
- Vue

Let's dig in!

1. React: The Component-Based Powerhouse

React is a Javascript library designed with components in mind! It provides a framework where you can make individual pieces that are combined to build the larger function. This is now the most common framework. It's maintained by Facebook.

With React, you focus on breaking down your UI into reusable components, making your code much easier to manage and reason about.

What React does:

- Component-based system
- Huge support in the community
- Can be used to make interactive websites that are fast and efficient

However, learning React can be a full-time project in itself.

A Personal Insight: I highly advise looking into this when you want to up your coding ability. There are few more impactful methods than learning how to use React effectively.

2. Angular: The Comprehensive Framework

Angular is a platform and framework for building client applications with HTML, CSS and Javascript/Typescript. Angular is different because the framework defines how you build everything from the architecture to the testing. It's mostly maintained by Google.

It's less popular than React, but still very commonly found.

What Angular does:

- Opinionated approach to create applications
- Less flexible
- A good start if you want to become a web developer

A Personal Insight: While extremely powerful, learning Angular can take quite a lot of effort, especially given the fast-paced web industry.

3. Vue: The Progressive Framework

Vue is described as a progressive framework because it's designed to be adaptable and versatile for Javascript needs. Its core library focuses on the view layer only. Vue has a relatively gentle learning curve which has made it a popular choice for single-page applications (SPAs) and interactive components.

What Vue does:

- Simple to understand
- Can be applied progressively
- Great option for those smaller projects.

A Personal Insight: I am now learning Vue to experiment with and see how its strengths can be brought to bear.

9.4 When to Use a Library (and When Not To) – Making the Right Choice

JavaScript libraries can be a valuable tool for web developers, but it's important to use them wisely. In the current JavaScript landscape it's often best to not use jQuery, due to the simplicity in selecting DOMs.

Here are some factors to consider when deciding whether to use a library:

- **Complexity of the Project:** If you're building a complex web application, a library can save you a significant amount of time and effort.
- **Team Size:** If you're working on a team, using a library can help to ensure consistency and code quality.
- **Learning Curve:** Libraries typically have a learning curve. Consider the time it will take to learn the library and whether it's worth the investment.
- **Performance:** Libraries can add overhead to your web page, potentially affecting performance. Consider the size of the library and the impact it will have on your page load time.

Here are some guidelines for when to use a library (and when not to):

- **Use a library when:**
  - You need to perform a complex task that is already well-solved by a library.
  - You want to improve the quality and maintainability of your code.
  - You're working on a team and need to ensure consistency.
- **Avoid using a library when:**
  - You can easily accomplish the task with native JavaScript.
  - You're concerned about performance or page load time.
  - You're just starting out and want to learn the fundamentals of JavaScript.

A Personal Insight: I always try to start with native JavaScript whenever possible, and only bring in a library if I need to solve a problem that is too complex or time-consuming to solve on my own. This helps me to keep my code lean and efficient and to avoid becoming overly reliant on external dependencies.

Conclusion: An Overview of Libraries

You've now explored the world of JavaScript libraries, from the classic jQuery library to the modern frameworks like React, Angular, and Vue. You've gained an understanding of what libraries are, how they can help you, and when to use them (and when not to). Remember that libraries are just tools, and it's important to choose the right tool for the job. With a good understanding of JavaScript fundamentals and a willingness to explore new technologies, you'll be well-equipped to build amazing web applications that push the boundaries of what's possible. You have more resources at your disposal than ever.

Chapter 10: Putting It All Together: Mini-Projects – Unleashing Your Creativity

You've journeyed through the core concepts and tools of JavaScript, and now it's time to harness your knowledge and build tangible projects! This chapter is all about turning theory into practice, transforming abstract concepts into interactive experiences, and solidifying your understanding through hands-on application. Think of these mini-projects as your training ground, where you can experiment, make mistakes, and learn from your experiences.

These projects will give you the opportunity to apply everything you've learned so far: DOM manipulation, event handling, functions, arrays, objects, and asynchronous JavaScript. By the end of this chapter, you'll have a collection of projects to show off your abilities. Let's get started.

General Approach to Each Project:

For each project, we'll follow a structured approach:

1. **Project Description:** A brief overview of the project's functionality and purpose.
2. **Planning:** Breaking down the project into smaller, manageable tasks.
3. **HTML Structure:** Creating the basic HTML structure for the project.
4. **CSS Styling:** Adding CSS styles to enhance the visual appearance of the project.
5. **JavaScript Implementation:** Writing the JavaScript code to add interactivity and functionality.
6. **Enhancements (Optional):** Ideas for extending the project and adding more features.

10.1 Project 1: Interactive Image Gallery – Bringing Images to Life

- **Project Description:** Create an interactive image gallery that displays a set of images and allows the user to navigate through them using navigation buttons or thumbnails.
- **Planning:**
    1. Create an HTML structure for the image gallery with a main image area, navigation buttons, and thumbnails.
    2. Add CSS styles to position and style the elements.
    3. Use JavaScript to:
        - Load the images into an array.
        - Display the first image in the main image area.
        - Update the main image when the user clicks on a navigation button or thumbnail.
- **HTML Structure:**
- `<div class="gallery-container">`

- `<img id="main-image" src="" alt="Main Image">`
- `<div class="navigation">`
- `<button id="prev-btn">Previous</button>`
- `<button id="next-btn">Next</button>`
- `</div>`
- `<div class="thumbnails">`
- `</div>`

`</div>`

- **CSS Styling:** (Basic Example)
- `.gallery-container {`
- `width: 600px;`
- `margin: 0 auto;`
- `}`
- `#main-image {`
- `width: 100%;`
- `}`
- `.thumbnails {`
- `display: flex;`
- `justify-content: space-around;`
- `}`
- `.thumbnails img {`
- `width: 80px;`
- `cursor: pointer;`

`}`

- **JavaScript Implementation:**
- `const images = ["image1.jpg", "image2.jpg", "image3.jpg"]; // Replace with your image paths`
- `let currentImageIndex = 0;`

- `const mainImage = document.getElementById("main-image");`
- `const prevBtn = document.getElementById("prev-btn");`
- `const nextBtn = document.getElementById("next-btn");`
- `const thumbnailsContainer = document.querySelector(".thumbnails");`
-
- `function updateMainImage() {`
- `mainImage.src = images[currentImageIndex];`
- `}`

```
// Create thumbnails
images.forEach((image, index) => {
  const img = document.createElement("img");
  img.src = image;
  img.addEventListener("click", () => {
    currentImageIndex = index;
    updateMainImage();
  });
  thumbnailsContainer.appendChild(img);
});


// Navigation Buttons
prevBtn.addEventListener("click", () => {
  currentImageIndex = (currentImageIndex - 1 + images.length) %
images.length;
  updateMainImage();
});


nextBtn.addEventListener("click", () => {
  currentImageIndex = (currentImageIndex + 1) % images.length;
  updateMainImage();
});


updateMainImage(); // Initial display
```

- **Enhancements (Optional):**
  - Add image descriptions.
  - Implement a slideshow feature.
  - Use CSS transitions to create smoother animations.

A Personal Insight: The image gallery project is a great way to practice DOM manipulation, event handling, and working with arrays. It also provides an opportunity to enhance your CSS skills and create visually appealing user interfaces.

10.2 Project 2: Simple Quiz Application – Testing Knowledge

- **Project Description:** Create a simple quiz application that presents the user with a series of multiple-choice questions and tracks their score.

- **Planning:**
    1. Create an HTML structure for the quiz application with a question area, answer options, and a submit button.
    2. Add CSS styles to format the quiz elements.
    3. Use JavaScript to:
        - Store the quiz questions and answers in an array of objects.
        - Display the first question and answer options.
        - Check the user's answer when they click on a submit button.
        - Provide feedback to the user (correct or incorrect).
        - Track the user's score.
        - Display the next question or the final score when the quiz is complete.
- **HTML Structure:**

```html
<div class="quiz-container">
  <h2 id="question">Question goes here</h2>
  <div id="answer-buttons">
    <button class="btn">Answer 1</button>
    <button class="btn">Answer 2</button>
    <button class="btn">Answer 3</button>
    <button class="btn">Answer 4</button>
  </div>
  <button id="next-button">Next</button>
</div>
```

- **CSS Styling:** (Basic Example)

```css
.quiz-container {
  width: 600px;
  margin: 0 auto;
}
.btn {
  display: block;
  width: 100%;
  margin-bottom: 10px;
}
```

- **JavaScript Implementation:**

```javascript
const questions = [
  {
    question: "What is 2 + 2?",
    answers: ["3", "4", "5", "6"],
```

```javascript
      correctAnswer: "4"
  },
  {
    question: "What is the capital of France?",
    answers: ["London", "Paris", "Berlin", "Rome"],
    correctAnswer: "Paris"
  }
];

let currentQuestionIndex = 0;
let score = 0;

const questionElement = document.getElementById("question");
const answerButtons = document.getElementById("answer-buttons");
const nextButton = document.getElementById("next-button");

function displayQuestion() {
  const currentQuestion = questions[currentQuestionIndex];
  questionElement.textContent = currentQuestion.question;

  answerButtons.innerHTML = ""; // Clear previous answers

  currentQuestion.answers.forEach(answer => {
    const button = document.createElement("button");
    button.classList.add("btn");
    button.textContent = answer;
    button.addEventListener("click", () => {
      if (answer === currentQuestion.correctAnswer) {
        score++;
      }
      nextQuestion();
    });
    answerButtons.appendChild(button);
  });
}

function nextQuestion() {
  currentQuestionIndex++;
  if (currentQuestionIndex < questions.length) {
```

```
        displayQuestion();
      } else {
        questionElement.textContent = `Quiz Complete! Your score: ${score}
  / ${questions.length}`;
        answerButtons.innerHTML = "";
        nextButton.style.display = "none";
      }
  }

  nextButton.addEventListener("click", () => {
    nextQuestion();
  });

  displayQuestion(); // Initial display
```

- **Enhancements (Optional):**
  - Add more questions.
  - Implement a timer.
  - Display different types of questions (e.g., multiple choice, true/false, short answer).
  - Store the user's high score in local storage.

A Personal Insight: The quiz application project is a fun way to practice working with arrays, objects, event handling, and DOM manipulation. It's also a good starting point for exploring more advanced web application development techniques.

10.3 Project 3: Basic To-Do List – Task Management

- **Project Description:** Create a basic to-do list application that allows the user to add, view, and remove tasks from a list.
- **Planning:**
  1. Create an HTML structure with input to add new items.
  2. Add CSS styles to look good.
  3. Use JavaScript to load the initial to-do list, then add the various functions and actions for editing the to-do list.
- **HTML Structure:**

```
<div id="todoContainer">
    <input type="text" id="taskInput" placeholder="Enter a task">
    <button id="addTask">Add Task</button>
    <ul id="taskList">
        <li>Example</li>
```

-     `</ul>`

   `</div>`

- **CSS Styling:** (Basic Example)

```css
/*Add style to the to-do list
*/
#todoContainer {
    border: 2px solid black;
    width: 500px;
}
ul {
    padding: 10px;
    text-align: left;
}
li {
    list-style-type: none;
}
```

- **JavaScript Implementation:**

```javascript
document.addEventListener('DOMContentLoaded', function() {
    const taskInput = document.getElementById('taskInput');
    const addTaskButton = document.getElementById('addTask');
    const taskList = document.getElementById('taskList');

    addTaskButton.addEventListener('click', function() {
        const taskText = taskInput.value.trim(); //Get value of entered task
        if (taskText !== '') { //Make sure task is not an empty string
            const taskItem = document.createElement('li'); //Create list element
            taskItem.textContent = taskText; //add the text to list element
            taskList.appendChild(taskItem); //add the new list item to the list
            taskInput.value = ''; // Reset the input
        } else {
            alert('Please enter a task!');
        }
    });
```

```
});
```

- **Enhancements (Optional):**
  - ○ Give user the ability to load information that persists.
  - ○ Marking elements as completed.

A Personal Insight: This project really focuses on all the building blocks that we've worked on. Using what we've learned we can create effective tools for day-to-day life.

10.4 Project 4: Dynamic Content Slider – Captivating Visuals

- **Project Description:** Create a dynamic content slider that displays a series of slides (images, text, or a combination of both) and allows the user to navigate through them using navigation controls.
- **Planning:**
  1. Create an HTML structure for the content slider with a container for the slides and navigation controls.
  2. Add CSS styles to position and style the slides and navigation controls.
  3. Use JavaScript to:
     - Load the slide content into an array.
     - Display the first slide.
     - Update the visible slide when the user clicks on a navigation control.
     - Implement a timer to automatically advance to the next slide.
- **HTML Structure:**

```html
<div class="slider-container">
    <div class="slider">
        <div class="slide">Slide 1 Content</div>
        <div class="slide">Slide 2 Content</div>
        <div class="slide">Slide 3 Content</div>
    </div>
    <div class="controls">
        <button id="prevSlide">Previous</button>
        <button id="nextSlide">Next</button>
    </div>
</div>
```

- **CSS Styling:** (Basic Example)

```css
.slider-container {
    width: 500px;
```

```css
    height: 300px;
    position: relative;
    overflow: hidden;
}

.slider {
    height: 100%;
    display: flex;
    transition: transform 0.5s ease-in-out;
}

.slide {
    width: 100%;
    height: 100%;
    flex-shrink: 0; /* Important for slider width */
    display: flex;
    justify-content: center;
    align-items: center;
    font-size: 2em;
    color: white;
    background-color: #333;
}
```

- **JavaScript Implementation:**

```javascript
document.addEventListener('DOMContentLoaded', function() {
    const slider = document.querySelector('.slider');
    const slides = document.querySelectorAll('.slide');
    const prevButton = document.getElementById('prevSlide');
    const nextButton = document.getElementById('nextSlide');

    let currentIndex = 0;
    const slideCount = slides.length;
    let slideWidth = slides[0].offsetWidth; // Get width dynamically

    //Adjust the slide width upon resizing
    window.addEventListener('resize', () => {
        slideWidth = slides[0].offsetWidth;
        updateSlider();
    });
```

```
    function updateSlider() {
        slider.style.transform = `translateX(-${currentIndex *
slideWidth}px)`;
    }

    prevButton.addEventListener('click', () => {
        currentIndex = (currentIndex - 1 + slideCount) % slideCount;
        updateSlider();
    });

    nextButton.addEventListener('click', () => {
        currentIndex = (currentIndex + 1) % slideCount;
        updateSlider();
    });
});
```

- **Enhancements (Optional):**
  - Implement a slideshow timer
  - Add indicators.
  - Allow touch and drag functionality.

A Personal Insight: Adding a dynamic slider can dramatically improve the visuals and engagement of websites. Understanding how to animate these web elements can make a huge difference.

10.5 Project 5: Interactive Form with Validation – Refined Data Input

- **Project Description:** Create an interactive form with validation that provides real-time feedback to the user as they fill out the form.
- **Planning:**
  1. Create an HTML structure for the form with various input fields and validation hints.
  2. Add CSS styles to design the form and the validation feedback.
  3. Use JavaScript to:
     - Validate each input field as the user types.
     - Display error messages for invalid input.
     - Enable the submit button only when all fields are valid.
- **HTML Structure:**

```html
<form id="signupForm">
    <label for="username">Username:</label>
    <input type="text" id="username" name="username" required>
```

- ```html
  <span id="usernameError" class="error"></span>
  ```
- ```html
  <label for="email">Email:</label>
  ```
- ```html
  <input type="email" id="email" name="email" required>
  ```
- ```html
  <span id="emailError" class="error"></span>
  ```
- ```html
  <label for="password">Password:</label>
  ```
- ```html
  <input type="password" id="password" name="password" required>
  ```
- ```html
  <span id="passwordError" class="error"></span>
  ```
- ```html
  <button type="submit">Sign Up</button>
  ```

```html
</form>
```

- **CSS Styling:** (Basic Example)
- ```css
  #signupForm {
  ```
- ```css
      width: 400px;
  ```
- ```css
      margin: 20px auto;
  ```
- ```css
      padding: 20px;
  ```
- ```css
      border: 1px solid #ccc;
  ```
- ```css
  }
  ```
-
- ```css
  #signupForm label {
  ```
- ```css
      display: block;
  ```
- ```css
      margin-top: 10px;
  ```
- ```css
  }
  ```
-
- ```css
  #signupForm input {
  ```
- ```css
      width: 100%;
  ```
- ```css
      padding: 8px;
  ```
- ```css
      margin-top: 5px;
  ```
- ```css
      margin-bottom: 10px;
  ```
- ```css
      box-sizing: border-box;
  ```
- ```css
  }
  ```
-
- ```css
  .error {
  ```
- ```css
      color: red;
  ```
- ```css
      font-size: 0.8em;
  ```
```css
  }
```

- **JavaScript Implementation:**
- ```javascript
  document.addEventListener('DOMContentLoaded', function() {
  ```
- ```javascript
      const form = document.getElementById('signupForm');
  ```

```javascript
const usernameInput = document.getElementById('username');
const emailInput = document.getElementById('email');
const passwordInput = document.getElementById('password');

const usernameError = document.getElementById('usernameError');
const emailError = document.getElementById('emailError');
const passwordError = document.getElementById('passwordError');

form.addEventListener('submit', function(event) {
    event.preventDefault();

    let isValid = true;

    if (usernameInput.value.length < 3) {
        usernameError.textContent = 'Username must be at least 3
characters long.';
        isValid = false;
    } else {
        usernameError.textContent = '';
    }

    if (!emailInput.value.includes('@')) {
        emailError.textContent = 'Enter a valid email address.';
        isValid = false;
    } else {
        emailError.textContent = '';
    }

    if (passwordInput.value.length < 8) {
        passwordError.textContent = 'Password must be at least 8
characters long.';
        isValid = false;
    } else {
        passwordError.textContent = '';
    }

    if (isValid) {
        alert('Form is valid and ready to submit!');
    }
```

- ```
  });
  ```
  ```
  });
  ```

- **Enhancements (Optional):**
  - Add more input fields and validation rules.
  - Implement real-time validation as the user types.
  - Use regular expressions for more complex validation patterns.
  - Provide more informative error messages.

A Personal Insight: Validating forms and being conscious of form types are critical in web development.

Conclusion: A New Journey

I congratulate you and hope you put these skills to use!
  ```

Conclusion: Next Steps – Your Web Development Adventure Awaits!

Congratulations! You've reached the end of "JavaScript: Powering the Web. A Visual Guide to Interactive Web Pages!" You've progressed from basic syntax to building interactive elements and dynamic web applications. You now have the tools needed to use JavaScript. However, this journey is far from over!

This conclusion provides a clear path forward, pointing you toward advanced resources, suggesting new learning avenues, and offering a glimpse into the ever-evolving world of JavaScript. Think of this as the launching pad for all your future web-based ambitions!

Key Takeaways and Next Steps – Building upon Your Foundation

Let's quickly recap what you've accomplished:

- o **Mastered JavaScript Fundamentals:** You understand variables, data types, control flow, functions, arrays, and objects.
- o **Conquered the DOM:** You know how to select, manipulate, and style HTML elements using JavaScript.
- o **Created Interactive Experiences:** You've learned to respond to user events and build engaging web applications.
- o **Familiarized Yourself with Key Libraries:** You have an overview of jQuery and modern frameworks like React, Angular, and Vue.
- o **Built Practical Projects:** You've applied your knowledge to create a portfolio of mini-projects.

So what's next? The key is to build upon that foundation and expand your skillset. Here are a few suggestions:

- o **Dive Deeper into Modern Frameworks:** Explore React, Angular, or Vue in more detail. These frameworks are used by many companies and offer powerful tools for building complex web applications.
- o **Learn About Backend Development:** Combine your JavaScript skills with a backend language like Node.js to build full-stack web applications.
- o **Explore Data Visualization Libraries:** Learn about libraries like D3.js or Chart.js to create interactive charts and graphs.
- o **Contribute to Open Source Projects:** Get involved in the JavaScript community and contribute to projects that interest you.

A Personal Insight: My JavaScript journey really took off when I started working on personal projects that I was passionate about. Find something that excites you and use JavaScript to bring it to life!

Resources for Further Learning – The Tools for Continued Growth

The internet is overflowing with resources to help you continue learning JavaScript. Here are a few of my favorites:

- **Mozilla Developer Network (MDN):** https://developer.mozilla.org/en-US/docs/Web/JavaScript – The MDN documentation is the most comprehensive and reliable resource for all things JavaScript.
- **freeCodeCamp:** https://www.freecodecamp.org/ – freeCodeCamp offers a vast library of coding challenges and projects.
- **Codecademy:** https://www.codecademy.com/learn/introduction-to-javascript – Codecademy provides interactive JavaScript courses that are perfect for beginners.
- **Stack Overflow:** https://stackoverflow.com/questions/tagged/javascript – Stack Overflow is an essential resource for finding answers to your JavaScript questions.

A Personal Insight: Don't be afraid to Google! Every developer, including me, spends a lot of time searching for answers online. The key is to learn how to effectively search for information and to evaluate the credibility of different sources.

The Future of JavaScript – A Dynamic Landscape

The JavaScript landscape is constantly evolving, with new features, libraries, and frameworks emerging all the time. Here are a few trends to watch out for:

- **WebAssembly (WASM):** WASM is a new binary instruction format that allows you to run code written in other languages (like C++ or Rust) in the browser with near-native performance. This could revolutionize web development by enabling more complex and performance-intensive applications to run in the browser.
- **Serverless Computing:** Serverless computing allows you to run JavaScript code on servers without managing the underlying infrastructure. This can simplify web development and make it easier to scale your applications.
- **AI-Powered Development Tools:** AI is being used to create new tools that can help developers write code more efficiently and effectively, such as code completion, bug detection, and automated testing.

A Personal Insight: The future of JavaScript is bright. The language is constantly evolving, and new technologies are emerging that are pushing the boundaries of what's possible in web development. Embrace the change, stay curious, and never stop learning.

You are now ready for a long-term path in Javascript!

Appendix A: JavaScript Syntax Cheat Sheet

[This appendix would provide a quick reference guide to JavaScript syntax, including:

- Variables: `let, const, var`
- Data Types: `number, string, boolean, object, array, null, undefined`
- Operators: `+, -, *, /, %, ==, ===, !=, !==, >, <, >=, <=, &&, ||, !`
- Control Flow: `if, else if, else, for, while, break, continue`
- Functions: `function, return, arguments, arrow functions`
- Objects: Object literals, dot notation, bracket notation, methods
- DOM Manipulation: `document.getElementById, document.querySelector, element.inner HTML, element.addEventListener`]

Appendix B: Setting Up Your Development Environment (VS Code, etc.)

[This appendix would provide detailed, step-by-step instructions for setting up a JavaScript development environment using VS Code, including:

- Installing VS Code
- Installing the Live Server extension
- Creating a new HTML file
- Linking a JavaScript file to the HTML file
- Opening the HTML file in a web browser]

Glossary of JavaScript Terms

[This appendix would define key JavaScript terms:]

- **Asynchronous:** A programming model where operations can run concurrently without blocking the main thread.
- **Callback:** A function passed as an argument to another function, to be executed when that function completes.
- **DOM (Document Object Model):** A programming interface for HTML and XML documents, representing the document as a tree structure.
- **Event:** An action or occurrence that happens in the browser, such as a click, mouseover, or form submission.
- **Function:** A reusable block of code that performs a specific task.
- **Library:** A collection of pre-written code that provides commonly used functions, objects, and tools.
- **Object:** A data structure that stores data as key-value pairs.
- **Promise:** An object representing the eventual completion (or failure) of an asynchronous operation.
- **Scope:** The region of a program where a variable is accessible.

- **Variable:** A name that refers to a memory location where data is stored.